How To Play The Harmonica

A Beginner's Guide to Learning The Basics of Playing The Harmonica

JENSON GREEN

© Copyright 2020 - All rights reserved.

The content contained within this book may not be reproduced, duplicated or transmitted without direct written permission from the author or the publisher.

Under no circumstances will any blame or legal responsibility be held against the publisher, or author, for any damages, reparation, or monetary loss due to the information contained within this book, either directly or indirectly.

Legal Notice:

This book is copyright protected. It is only for personal use. You cannot amend, distribute, sell, use, quote or paraphrase any part, or the content within this book, without the consent of the author or publisher.

Disclaimer Notice:

Please note the information contained within this document is for educational and entertainment purposes only. All effort has been executed to present accurate, up to date, reliable, complete information. No warranties of any kind are declared or implied. Readers acknowledge that the author is not engaged in the rendering of legal, financial, medical or professional advice. The content within this book has been derived from various sources. Please consult a licensed professional before attempting any techniques outlined in this book.

By reading this document, the reader agrees that under no circumstances is the author responsible for any losses, direct or indirect, that are incurred as a result of the use of the information contained within this document, including, but not limited to, errors, omissions, or inaccuracies.

Table of Contents

Introduction 1

Chapter 1: Getting to Know the Harmonica 4
    How a Harmonica Works 6
        How to Choose a Harmonica 10

Chapter 2: Getting Started with the Harmonica 14
    Shopping for Harmonicas and Making Your First Sounds 18
        Playing Notes and Reading Tabs - Getting Started on Your Harmonica 21

Chapter 3: Techniques for Playing 26
    Bending 29
        Tips and Tricks for Bends, Hand Positions, and Other Playing Techniques 31

Chapter 4: Playing in Different Positions 38
    Positions and Modes on a Diatonic C Harmonica 41
        When and Why to Change Position 45

Chapter 5: Your Musical Style 49
    Harmonica Tabs for Classic Rock 53
    Harmonica Tabs for Traditional Songs 58

Chapter 6: Building a Collection 67
    Starting Your Collection 70
        Recommended Harmonicas for Different Requirements 72

Chapter 7: Cleaning and Maintaining Your Harmonica 76
    Tuning and Cleaning Your Harmonica 79
        Tips, Tricks, and Common Mistakes to Avoid when Cleaning Your Harmonica 81

Chapter 8: Glossary of Terms 84
    A-M 84
    N-Z 86

Conclusion 89

References 90

Introduction

Leao, R. (n.d.). *pencil on printing paper* [Photograph]. Unsplash. https://unsplash.com/photos/k4WJjF0-3Yo

If you can breathe, you can play harmonica. - Aishwary Sharma

When we hear the harmonica, we think of the southern and western United States. We think of blues and bayous, open plains, deserts, and cowboys. It's a versatile instrument that appears in a wide variety of genres, but it's also relatively understated. Many of us receive harmonicas in our Christmas stockings or as birthday presents as young children, but few people choose to pursue it more seriously.

This book is a comprehensive introduction to one of the most ubiquitous instruments in American music. Whether you have your heart set on learning the harmonica or are searching for an instrument to pursue, this book will give you a basic introduction to the instrument's history, the different genres it appears in, and the many different kinds of harmonicas out there for you to choose from. This book will also act as an instruction manual, walking you through the basics of how to play the harmonica, how to read the music that's written for it, and how to properly care for your instrument. If you've received a harmonica as a gift or are shy about taking a music class, you've come to the right place. With this book in hand, you can learn everything you need to begin playing your own music from the comfort of your own home.

From the very beginning, the harmonica is an instrument that's meant to be played. Its popularity in American folk genres like blues or rock and roll comes from the fact that it's *not* an instrument you need classical training to master. If you have no musical talent or training, don't worry. You stand in a long tradition of masterful harmonica players who never once set foot in a classroom. This is an instrument that's easy to play and beautiful to listen to. This is an instrument that's made for any person, no matter what kind of education, training, or music they're trying to play. Don't let its looks, beauty, or versatility intimidate you. With the right guidance, the harmonica is a very easy instrument to master. This book will show you how best to play, including how to shape your mouth and position your body. You'll learn which harmonicas are best for different genres, and learn how to play all the many musical styles of harmonica to find the one that's right for you. All you need to master this instrument is a little bit of basic instruction, and with this book in hand, you have that instruction without ever having to leave your home.

I am something of a music enthusiast. When I'm not playing music, I'm listening to it. I play many different instruments, but the harmonica is easily one of my favorites. It's one of the few instruments that manages to be both versatile and simple. I can play the same instrument in bands of three very different genres, and it's small enough to fit in my pocket!

I first encountered the harmonica the way that most people do—as a gift. This was specifically a Christmas gift from my uncle five years ago. When I received this gift, I didn't consider myself a musician at all. But I loved to listen to music, especially jazz and blues, and would proudly show off my collection of blues records to anyone visiting my apartment. I think gifting me with a was intended to acknowledge my love for the blues and support my interest. I don't think anyone expected me to start playing it seriously. But five years later, it's one of my favorite instruments.

With this book, I'm giving you the same gift that my uncle gave to me—music. The harmonica opened up an entirely new world of music for me, the world of the musician. Learning the harmonica taught me the deep joy of playing an instrument, and gave me the confidence to get onstage and experience music as the player, and not just the listener. Since then, I've gone on to master many more instruments, but the harmonica holds a special place in my heart because it was my first.

No one taught me how to play the harmonica. I didn't attend classes or watch instructional videos. I taught myself, slowly but surely, by experimenting with the instrument on my own and listening to how other people play. This book will synthesize all of the information that I learned the hard way so that you can benefit from my mistakes. The techniques that I developed for myself will work for you, too, so that you can buy your own harmonica and start playing without having to worry about paying for lessons.

I'm sharing this book with you because I want you to feel the joy that I felt when I realized that learning a musical instrument didn't have to be difficult or scary. Music isn't something for an elite group of talented or wealthy people—it's something that anyone can do! When you read this book, my hope for you is that you experience the same joy and confidence that the harmonica gave to me. No matter what kind of musical background or training you have, this is an instrument that you can easily master on your own. And who knows? Perhaps this book will encourage you to experiment with other instruments in the future.

Right now, the harmonica is something that you've seen and heard before, but you've never tried to play yourself. It's a mystery, just another instrument that you don't know how to play. But once you've finished this book, you'll never look at the harmonica the same way again. You'll know its many different parts and all the different types. You'll understand the basic techniques for playing this instrument, and you'll have insight into how to choose one for yourself. You'll be familiar with the many different genres and styles the harmonica can play, and once you've purchased your own, you'll understand exactly how to clean and care for it. Right now, you're a novice, a beginner. But by the end of this book, you'll be purchasing an instrument of your own and playing your own songs. You may not have any musical training at all, but by the end of this book, you'll be a musician.

Chapter 1:
Getting to Know the Harmonica

Most of us have seen or heard a harmonica before. Perhaps you've even seen someone play it live or know someone who can play. But how much do you *really* know about this instrument?

The harmonica is officially classified as an "aerophone" or a free reed wind instrument. In other words, the harmonica is an instrument that is played by blowing into the instrument. Like the flute (another aerophone), it doesn't need a reed to make a sound. Though it's an extremely tiny instrument, it's makeup is surprisingly complex. The harmonica comprises five basic parts: the comb, the reed-plate, the cover plate, the windsavers, and the mouthpiece.

The **comb** is the main body of the instrument, housing the air chambers that cover the reeds inside. It gets its name from its similarity in shape and size to a common hair comb. Traditional harmonica combs were made from wood, but today they are most likely to be made from plastic or metal. Though they look simple, many modern designs are quite complex in how they direct the flow of air. When the first metal harmonicas were manufactured, this caused a bit of controversy among purists, who were concerned that changing the comb's material would also change the nature of the sound. And while there are differences in the sounds made by wood, metal, and plastic harmonicas, these differences are extremely subtle.

However, wooden combs absorb moisture from the player's breath and tongue, while metal and plastic ones do not. This can cause the entire instrument to expand slightly, making it very uncomfortable to play. Despite this momentary expansion, wood combs shrink over time. This can lead to cracks that prevent the harmonica from making sounds. The restoration of wood combs is an ongoing project for those who prefer to play wooden harmonicas. Traditional players would soak their wood combs in water to encourage them to expand. Though these problems are less common in contemporary wood combs, metal and plastic combs are much more stable (Chrapka, 2018).

Though the harmonica is classified as a "free reed" instrument, it does rely on an internal fixture called a **reed plate,** which is essentially a group of many, tiny reeds bound tightly together. Most harmonicas are designed so that only one reed vibrates at a time, with different vibration frequencies producing different notes.

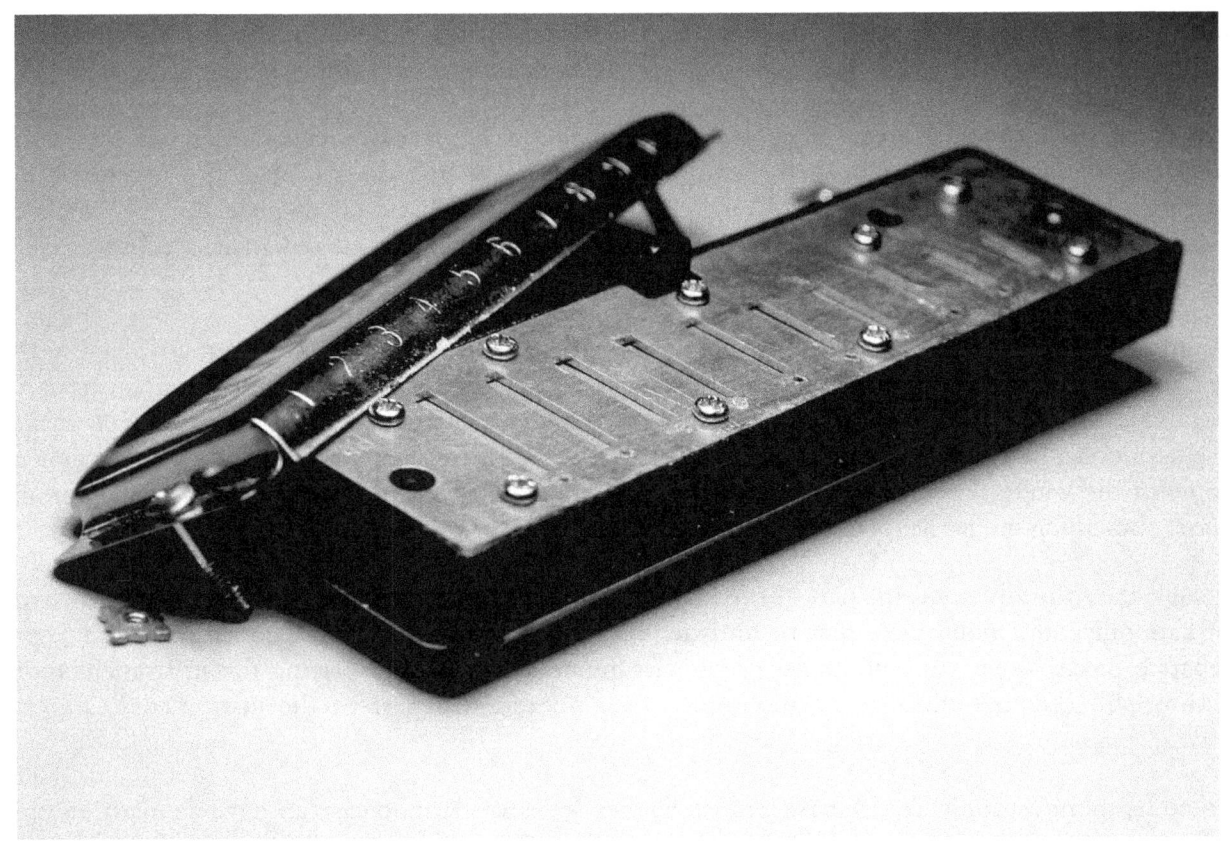

meineresterampe. (n.d.). *harmonica music inner working* [Photograph]. Pixabay. https://pixabay.com/photos/harmonica-music-inner-workings-352734/

If you were to open up the harmonica, you would see a sheet of yellowish metal. This is the reed plate. You would see several long strips of brass, steel, aluminum, or plastic, on top of the plate, which are the reeds themselves. Beneath the reeds are a series of rectangular openings. These openings are designed to mimic the shape of the reeds themselves. However, the openings are just a tiny bit larger than the reed, leaving a narrow opening of space to the left, right, and top of the reed. When you blow into the harmonica or suck your breath inward, air flows through these tiny openings and causes the reed to vibrate, producing the note.

The individual reeds are T-shaped. If you look at the reed plate, the spots where reeds are visible and where they aren't visible will alternate. In spots where they are not visible, the reed is simply facing the opposite direction. The reeds alternate according to whether they are designed to produce "blow" notes or "draw" notes. The reeds visible from the top are "draw" notes, meaning that they only produce sound when you suck (or draw) air into your mouth, while the reeds on the bottom are "blow" notes, meaning that they only produce sound when you blow air into the harmonica. The blow and draw reeds are lined up in an alternating pattern, according to the musical scale. C, E, and G are blow notes, while D, F, A, and B are draw notes. The harmonica is built this way, so you don't have to move your mouth up and down the mouthpiece profusely when you play. Rather than taking frequent breaks to inhale, you can produce notes whether you're blowing into the instrument or taking a deep breath in. As a harmonica player, you essentially learn to adjust your breathing patterns to quite literally make music (*The structure of the harmonica: Learn the names of the parts,* n.d.).

The **cover plate** covers the reeds to protect them and is usually made of metal, though it is sometimes made of wood or plastic. Unlike the comb, the plate's material does change the nature of the harmonica's sound. In addition to the material, there are two basic cover plate designs (open or closed), which also changes the harmonica's sound quality. The closed design is a more modern invention, while the open design is the traditional method.

Windsavers are tiny valves made from strips of plastic, paper, leather, or Teflon that are glued to the reedplate and direct the flow of air to and from the reeds. These are only found in certain types of harmonicas and are not part of the traditional design. The presence of the winsavers essentially makes the harmonica more airtight, and therefore much easier to play. When you blow into the harmonica, some of the windsavers are blown shut, preventing air from escaping from the harmonica in atonal ways. Something similar happens when you suck air in.

Finally, the **mouthpiece** is the part of the harmonica where you put your lips. Depending on the type of harmonica, the mouthpiece may be an extension of the comb, part of the cover plate, or its own separate piece. Today, the mouthpiece's primary function is to make playing the instrument more comfortable, but traditionally, the mouthpiece was an essential part of the instrument (Chrapka, 2018a).

Some harmonicas don't have windsavers, and other styles of harmonicas can have as many as nine different pieces, but these five parts form almost any harmonica you can find. Every time you blow air into the harmonica or draw air out of it, all five of these pieces work together in specific ways to produce the many notes of the musical scale.

How a Harmonica Works

At first glance, the harmonica is deceptively simple—you blow into the little box, and sound comes out. But how exactly is that sound made?

Unlike other wind instruments, harmonicas respond when you inhale and exhale. By changing the shape of your mouth, the placement of your tongue, the pressure of your breathing, and opening or closing your throat, you can change the notes, pitch, and tone of the harmonica's sound. The more you play, the more skilled you will become at changing the quality of the instrument's sound to reflect your personal expressive style.

Though they're often referred to as "harps," harmonicas are more similar to a pipe organ or an accordion, but rather than using a keyboard to direct the flow of air through the instrument, you place your mouth over the designated holes. The actual sound of the harmonica comes from the reeds. Each note has a specific reed that vibrates when you blow into or draw air from the corresponding hole. The way that the reeds are arranged inside the body of the harmonica determines whether they respond to when you exhale or inhale.

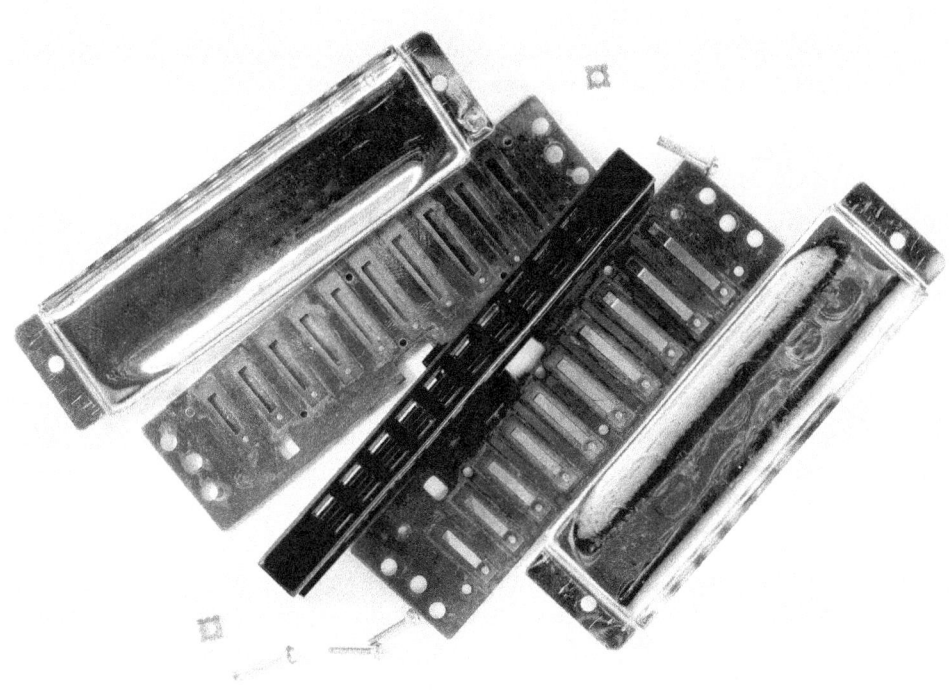

tOOn_in. (n.d.). *separate harmonica parts for repair and cleaning* [Photograph]. Shuttershock. https://www.shutterstock.com/image-photo/separate-harmonica-parts-repair-cleaning-788128441

Think of a harmonica as a mechanical five-layer sandwich, with each different part resting one on top of the next. The arrangement of these layers is what makes it possible for the harmonica to make music. The comb is the central layer. It has 10 individual grooves cut into its main body. These grooves give the comb its name, as the dividers between each opening look like the teeth of a common hair comb. The openings in the comb surround the reeds and direct the flow of air from your mouth to play different musical notes.

The two layers above and below the comb are the reed plates. The top reed plate houses the blow reeds, while the bottom one is for the draw reeds. Ten reeds are mounted to each reed plate to correspond with the ten openings carved into the comb. If you were to take off the top cover and look down into the harmonica, you wouldn't see the reeds themselves. This is because both reed plates are fastened to the comb with their reeds facing down.

Finally, the outermost layer of the harmonica is the cover plate. The cover plate is typically two separate pieces that are nailed together, forming a hollow chamber that transforms the reeds' vibrations into musical notes. The covers also make it possible for you to hold the harmonica without damaging the reeds. The cover plate is made of a thin, shiny metal that gives harmonicas their distinctive shine. Typically, harmonica covers are made from stainless steel, but sometimes they are made of brass that is then plated over with a layer of chrome or nickel.

The reeds are very thin strips of brass that vibrate within the body of the harmonica whenever you blow into it or draw air through it. One end of the reed is attached to the reed plate to hold it in place. The rest of it sits freely, not touching anything else so that it can vibrate. This is what classifies the harmonica as a "free reed" instrument (Chrapka, 2018b).

A series of tiny slots are carved into the reed plate itself to give the reeds enough space to swing up and down when air passes through the instrument. As the size of the reeds increase, so do the size of the slots around them. Each reed sticks up slightly from the reed plate. Air from your breath pushes the reed down, and then it naturally springs back up. This is what causes the reed to vibrate. To produce just one note, the reeds in your harmonica vibrate at hundreds and sometimes even thousands of times per second (Yerxa, 2016).

Some reeds are designed to vibrate when you blow air into the harmonica, while others are designed to vibrate when you inhale. The blow reeds are located on the upper side of the reed plate. Every time you exhale, the air from your breath sets the blow reeds vibrating. Every time air enters the harmonica through the comb; this pushes the blow reeds deeper into their slots. When they spring back into place, this creates a vibration. The deeper the reeds are pushed into their slots, the more energy they have, and when they spring back into place, their vibrations will be much more frantic. This is why the harder you blow into the harmonica, the louder the sound it produces. Draw notes work the same way but in reverse. Since they are arranged facing down, blowing into the harmonica does nothing to change their position. But when you suck air back into your lungs, the flow of that air is what presses the draw notes back into their slots and sets them vibrating (Chrapka, 2018b).

However, it's not only the vibration of the reeds that produce musical notes. Unlike the strings of a guitar, the reeds themselves aren't producing a sound that's simply magnified by the body of the harmonica. If you were to remove the cover plates and pluck a reed with your finger, it would vibrate, but all you would hear is a tiny, metallic *ping*. But when the reeds vibrate inside their air slots, they chop at the stream of air moving through the harmonica. In this way, the harmonica works similarly to the way a siren works. The reeds function like springs that tightly control the movement of the air around them. There's only a very narrow space where the air passes between the reed and the reed plate. But as the reed starts to move up and down, it periodically opens and restricts airflow. This strict control of the air stream creates the harmonica's distinctive sound (Chrapka, 2018b).

The body of a harmonica is extremely small. Unlike a guitar or a violin, there's nothing inside the body of the harmonica that amplifies its sound. The resonance of the harmonica's notes come from the player's mouth, which is one reason why the harmonica is such a unique and personal instrument. This is also why the materials that the harmonica is made of have such little effect on the quality of its sound. While there may be tiny differences in tone depending on what materials are used, the biggest influence on the quality of the harmonica's sound is the player (Chrapka, 2018b).

The speed at which the reed vibrates determines its *pitch*. Pitch indicates how high or low a note sounds. Longer reeds vibrate more slowly, and therefore produce lower notes. The heavier the reed is, the slower it vibrates, and the lower the note it produces. Shorter reeds, on the other hand, vibrate much more quickly, and therefore produce higher notes. If you take a look at your harmonica's reed plate, you'll see that the reeds increase in size from long to short as you move left to right. This arranges the notes from low to high, just like the notes are arranged on a piano.

The technique used to change the pitch of a note during play is called a *bend*. To create a bend, you encourage both of the reeds in the note's designated hole to vibrate simultaneously. Changing the pitch of a draw note is called a "draw bend." Changing the pitch of a blow note is called a "blow bend." In a draw bend, the first note that sounds is the draw note, then both reeds are set to vibrating, and finally, only the blow note is making a sound. A blow bend works the same way but in reverse. Bending can lower (or "bend") the pitch of the high note just one-half step above the low note.

To initiate a bend, the player uses the power of their breath to encourage both the original reed and its opposite pair to move together. For example, during a draw bend, the force of the player's breath causes the opposing reed (the blow reed) to move while the draw note makes sounds. When the comb's resonance is just right, this movement will give the blow note the energy that it needs to start vibrating. Traditionally, the movement of the reeds into their slots is called a "closing" note, while the movement of the reeds as they spring up out of their slots is an "opening" note. If this all sounds a bit confusing, don't worry! The physics of how the reeds move within a harmonica is relatively unexplored. Even experienced players don't quite understand how it all works; they know what to do with their mouths and breathe to make it happen.

An even more advanced technique is called an *overbend*. This technique is similar to playing a chord on a piano or guitar. In an overbend, both reeds in a designated hole are encouraged to vibrate together, playing two different notes at once. When you want to stop the chord from sounding, you employ a technique called "choking the reed," which gently forces one of the reeds back into its slot without causing it to vibrate. With the reed back in place, the harmonica goes back to playing just one note at a time (Chrapka, 2018b).

The notes on every harmonica are arranged the same way, just as the notes on every piano or guitar are always the same. Most harmonicas are C harmonicas, which means that the blow note for hole 4 is tuned to C. The next note up the scale (D) is the draw note for the same hole. This works no matter what note your harmonica is tuned to. So on an F-harp, for example, the blow note in hole 4 is F, and the next note up the scale (G), is the draw note in the same hole. Once you learn the musical notes on one harmonica, you can pick up any harmonica in the world and play it, just as people who play the guitar can pick up any guitar in the world and play it.

Most harmonicas have 10 holes, with the number appearing above each hole. Each hole has two different notes: the blow note and the draw note. In a C-harp, the blow notes for each hole (starting with hole 1 and ending with hole 10) are C, E, G, C, E, G, C, E, G, C. The draw notes for each hole are D, G, B, D, F, A, B, D, F, A (Yerxa, 2016).

How to Choose a Harmonica

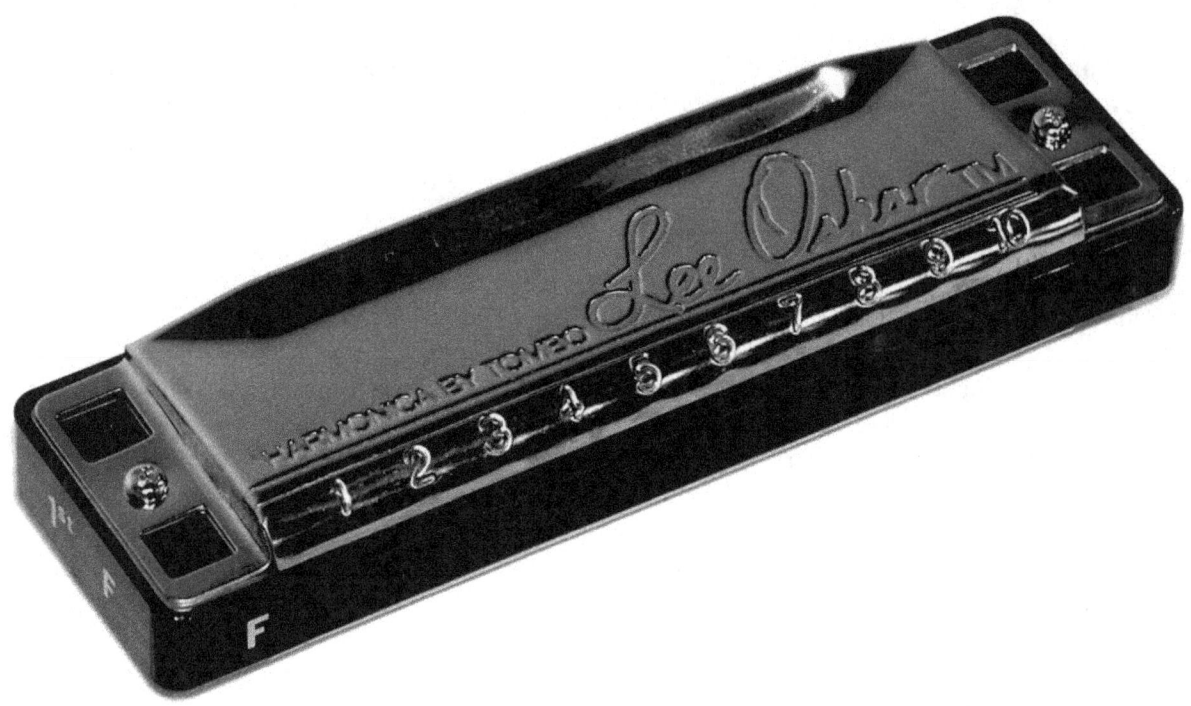

eurok. (n.d.). *harmonica* [Photograph]. FreeImages. https://www.freeimages.com/photo/harmonica-1558929

It's difficult to find a musical instrument that can top the playability and affordability of the harmonica. Considering both its size and cost, the harmonica is easily one of the most versatile instruments you can play. Though they most often appear in blues and country music, they can be used greatly in rock, jazz, and even classical music, too. Because of its wide usage, different styles of harmonicas have been developed over the years to create new and interesting sounds. All harmonicas contain the five basic parts. All of them are played by blowing and drawing. And all of them contain reeds that vibrate at certain frequencies to make notes. But these are just the basics. Over the years, experienced players have invented new techniques (like overbends) to produce sounds that the harmonica wasn't originally intended to make. Slight variations on the harmonica's inner structure can produce a very different quality of sound that's favored by different styles and genres. So whether you're an absolute beginner, or an experienced player looking to expand your options, you have a few things to consider when purchasing a harmonica that's right for you.

The first major point of variation from harmonica to harmonica is the materials used to build it. Combs are traditionally made from wood, but they can also be made of metal or plastic. Reeds are typically made from brass, but they can also be made from steel, aluminum, or plastic. Though these are the main components of a harmonica, differences in materials don't change its sound that much. Harmonicas with wooden combs sound almost exactly the same as harmonicas with metal ones. The material of the cover plate, on the other hand, is very important. Cover plates are most often made from metal, but they can also be made from wood or plastic, which dramatically changes the instrument's tonal quality (*How a Harmonica Works*, 2019).

All harmonicas, regardless of materials used, can be divided into three basic categories: diatonic, chromatic, tremolo. Several specialty harmonicas fall outside of these three main categories, but these can be extremely difficult to learn and aren't typically suitable for beginners. Each of these varies based on the range of notes that it can play, and each is favored by different musical genres.

The **diatonic** harmonica is by far the most common style of harmonica you can find. If you've received a harmonica as a gift, it's most likely a diatonic. Diatonic harmonicas have 10 holes and get their name because they are designed only to play the notes in a diatonic scale, or a scale that only contains the notes in a specific key. For example, the C diatonic scale only contains the notes C, D, E, F, G, A, and B. This is opposed to a chromatic scale, which contains *all* possible notes, including tones and semitones. For example, the C chromatic scale contains the notes C, C#, D, D#, E, F, F#, G, G#, A, A#, and B.

In theory, if you wanted to play every single note in all 12 musical keys, you would need 12 different diatonic harmonicas, one for each key. However, if you master pitch changing techniques like bending, you can change the "key" in which you're playing and expand the musical range of this simple instrument. A few famous players, including Howard Levy and Carlos Del Junco, are celebrated for their ability to play chromatically using a standard, 10-hole harmonica. With that said, many serious harmonica players find themselves with a small collection of diatonic harmonicas, each tuned to a different key. This might make these harmonicas sound like a bad investment, but because their cost is inexpensive, many talented players simply find this easier than learning how to bend. As you become more comfortable on your own harmonica, you can choose to learn bending techniques or try your hand at a second harmonic with a new tuning.

Diatonic harmonicas are favored by pop and blues players. Blues musicians, in particular, prefer to play in what is called a "cross harp" position. Essentially, this means playing with a harmonica that's tuned to a perfect fourth below the key in which the music is composed. For example, if you're playing a song that's written in the key of C, you would use an F harmonica to play in cross harp. Blues music typically uses a pentatonic scale, so many blues musicians favor harmonicas tuned to the key of G, as this gives you easy access to the pentatonic notes in a C scale.

Though bending is one way to change the key your harmonica is in, certain positions of play can also enhance the musical range of a diatonic harmonica. For example, cupping your hands around the instrument and using your tongue to block and unblock holes is a technique that can create chord-like sounds. Many of these techniques will be covered in detail later in this book. As a beginner, these techniques won't be immediately useful. However, they allow you to expand your musical repertoire indefinitely without purchasing a new harmonica if you don't want to. And the simplicity of the diatonic harmonica makes it a great choice for those who are just starting out (*Best Harmonica Beginner's Guide with TOP 10 Harmonica Reviews 2020*, 2020).

If you feel that this is the right style for you, you'll probably encounter many variations on the diatonic harmonica as you begin shopping. A popular example is the Lee Oskar line of harmonicas. Though these harmonicas are "standard" 10-hole diatonic harmonicas, most of them are tuned to minor or other non-standard scales. If you're new to the world of music, it's probably best to stick with a standard key like C or F before branching out to more unusual keys or tunings.

The **chromatic** harmonica can also have 10 holes, but it sometimes contains 12 or even 16. These harmonicas get their name from a special button that makes it possible for the same instrument to play all 12 notes in the chromatic scale. When pressed, this button activates a sliding bar that plays the diatonic scale in the key that it's tuned in. When pushed, all the notes become sharpened, pushing the key of the harmonica one half-step higher. Using this "gear shift," you can theoretically learn to play any scale or tune on one single chromatic harmonica (*The Ultimate Guide to Harmonicas for Curious Newbies,* 2020).

The chromatic harmonica's musical versatility is made possible by using much larger reeds than those in diatonic harmonicas. However, because of their size, it's very difficult to bend or change the pitch of individual notes. The sounds produced by chromatic harmonicas tend to be much bigger and deeper, giving this harmonica the nickname "Mississippi saxophone" in certain blues circles.

Despite its affectionate blues nickname, this harmonica type is used most often by jazz and classical musicians. Musicians like Toots Thielman and Stevie Wonder have made it a popular alternative to the "standard" diatonic. Stevie Wonder, in particular, is recognized for his ability to bend the notes on a chromatic harmonica, which can be quite difficult to do.

If you are passionate about jazz or classical harmonica, then a chromatic may be the right choice for you. However, chromatic harmonicas are much more difficult to play than diatonic harmonicas. Many instructors recommend learning the basics on a diatonic, and then upgrading to a chromatic once you get more comfortable. Learning the positions on a diatonic will make the transition to a chromatic much easier. And while chromatics normally come tuned in the key of C or G, you can learn to play any music that uses a 12-tone scale on the same chromatic instrument (*How to Choose a Harmonica,* 2018).

Tremolo harmonicas, sometimes called "echo" harmonicas, are set up like diatonic harmonicas. They have double holes, each with two reeds tuned to the same note, one slightly sharp, and the other slightly flat. It gets its name from the distinctive, "trembling" sound that its double reeds produce when played. Despite their hauntingly beautiful sound, however, tremolo harmonicas are not very popular. This is because the range of sounds they can produce is extremely limited compared to standard chromatic and diatonic harmonicas. Chromatic tremolo harmonicas are almost exclusively found in Asian rock and pop music, while diatonic tremolo harmonicas are rarely heard outside of folk and pop music (*Best for Beginners: Exploring Three Hamonica Types,* n.d.). **Octave** harmonicas are a special type of tremolo harmonica, in which the two reeds are tuned an entire octave apart. These harmonicas are favored by folk and gospel players (*Octave harmonicas* n.d.).

While all of these harmonicas have slightly different sounds and musical abilities, any experienced harmonica player will tell you that the most important factor in the harmonica's sound is the player's mouth. Using the power of your breath, lips, and tongue, you can change the pitch of any note on any harmonica. Once you've mastered the basics of how to position your lips, you can move on to bending and overbending to expand your musical ability on your own instrument. Sometimes called "overblowing," these techniques can be applied to any style of harmonica. Those who have mastered bending can play their harmonica in all 12 keys, regardless of the instrument's physical set-up or original musical limitations (*How a Harmonica Works*, 2019).

No matter which harmonica you choose, the best beginner harmonica is one on which you can successfully learn the skill of blowing and sucking the notes and placing your lips in the correct places. This way, if you choose to move on to more complicated models in the future, the additional skills that these harmonicas require can easily be acquired on top of your basic, foundational skill set.

Chapter 2:
Getting Started with the Harmonica

Hurley, S. (n.d.). *picture of harmonica on sheet music* [Photograph]. Burst. https://burst.shopify.com/photos/harmonica-on-sheet-music?q=harmonica

Now that you have a basic idea of how a harmonica works, it's time to choose your first instrument. C harmonicas are the most common, appearing in blues, folk, and rock music. Fortunately, if you're new to music theory, these are the easiest to learn on. Due to their popularity, they're also incredibly easy to find. Any local music store or reputable online shop will have at least a few different harmonicas for you to look at.

A diatonic harmonica tuned in the key of C is the recommended way to learn the basics of the harmonica. If you want to branch into different genres or more complicated harmonicas, it will be much easier to do so after mastering the basics. Most of the instruction and lessons in this book will assume that this is the kind of harmonica you have. Tremolo harmonicas are extremely difficult to learn (even if they have 10 holes), and so should be avoided if you are a beginner. The instruction in this book isn't appropriate for tremolo harmonicas, as they require slightly different techniques to be played properly. Even those who are more musically inclined should learn how to play a standard diatonic before learning a tremolo. While a 10 hole chromatic harmonica may not be a bad choice if you have your heart set on learning jazz harmonica, the reality is that these kinds of harmonicas are not beginner-friendly either. If you are an absolute beginner, it's best to stick with a diatonic harmonica for now. Remember that you can always upgrade in the future after you feel more comfortable.

While there are hundreds of harmonicas available for purchase, if you're a beginner, it's best to find something between $35 and $60. Anything cheaper than $35 is likely to be poorly constructed, causing them to leak air. This, in turn, makes them extremely difficult to play. It can also make it difficult to learn important techniques like bending. The same is true for "free" harmonicas that are included in book and instrument bundles. It may seem like a good deal, but the harmonicas in these packages are typically "free" because they're poorly made. You already have all the instruction you need with this book, so there's no reason to settle for an instrument that's going to inhibit your ability to learn. Unless your ambitions are extremely casual, try to keep the price tag on your instrument above $35.

I would only recommend buying a used harmonica if it was a gift or a hand-me-down from a serious player. Used harmonicas are a potential health hazard, especially if you don't know how to clean a harmonica properly. This is especially true if the harmonica in question has a wood comb. It's also not a necessary purchase, as a brand new instrument will only cost you around $35. Even the most meticulously cared-for harmonica will wear out over time. If you're just starting, you'll want to feel confident that your instrument is in good condition and plays in tune (*Which Harmonicas to Buy,* n.d.).

When shopping for your harmonica, try to find one with the numbers printed above each of the holes. The **Seydel Session Standard** and **Suzuki Harpmaster** are two specific types of harmonicas that are well-made, beginner-friendly, and very affordable. Hohner harmonicas will be a bit pricer than other brands, but you can trust that you've chosen a high-quality instrument that will last you a long time. Many Hohner harmonicas come with wood combs, but they are so well-made that they don't typically exhibit the usual problems associated with wood combs. However, when in doubt it's best to start with a harmonica with a metal or plastic comb. If you're stuck, find a harmonica that will run you under $40, and upgrade when you feel comfortable moving on to a different key.

There are a few specific harmonicas that I've found to be the best for beginning players. These harmonicas are not only beginner-friendly, but they're so well-made that you can continue to use them far beyond the beginner level if you wish. And though they're very high quality, none of these harmonicas will cost you an exorbitant amount of money. So if you're feeling overwhelmed while you browse, keep an eye out for these specific harmonica models (Whitner, 2020):

Hohner Special 20

Hohner is an extremely reputable harmonica manufacturer, and this instrument, in particular, is a great choice for beginning and advanced players alike. It's this harmonica that John Popper plays when he performs with the Blues Traveler, so it's an instrument that you can potentially play forever if you like the feel and sound. The comb is made of plastic, protected by steel covers on both sides. Remember, though a plastic comb may sound cheap, it's far more durable than wood. The reeds and the reed plates are made of brass. This is a great beginning harmonica because it's diatonic and tuned in the key of C. It has quite a loud sound, especially compared with other harmonicas, and so it is a great choice for those who would eventually like to play for an audience. And for the quality, it's extremely well priced. This is an excellent choice for beginners who expect that they will be playing for years into the future.

Hohner Special 20 Pros:

- Well-built;
- Easy to play;
- Recessed reed-plates, and;
- Stainless steel covers.

Hohner Special 20 Cons:

- Brass reed plates aren't as durable as other materials.

Lee Oskar Major Diatonic

This is another harmonica that's beginner-friendly, but the preferred instrument of many professional players, too. Lee Oskar, like Hohner, is a highly-respected harmonica manufacturer that has earned its reputation. This harmonica makes a great sound for blues and rock music. The mouth holes in this harmonica are slightly larger than is common, making it very comfortable to play. It also gives the harmonica a great deal of power, which is why it's such a good choice for rock and blues musicians, who often have drum-sets and guitar amps competing with them for sound on-stage. As it's tuned to the key of C, it's a perfect choice for the beginning player.

Lee Oskar Major Diatonic Pros:

- Made for blues and rock musicians;
- Very loud and comfortable to play;
- A plastic comb with largemouth holes, and;
- Airtight design.

Lee Oskar Major Diatonic Cons:

- Doesn't come with a carrying case

Fender Blues Deluxe

If you're familiar with guitars, you may recognize the manufacturer of this harmonica. And yes, it is the same Fender. The comb on this beautiful instrument is made of PVC and protected by a chromed metal layer. This is marketed as the perfect harmonica and is designed to be incredibly easy to play so that you can play for longer without feeling winded. Tuned in the key of C, it's appropriate for beginners, but so well made that you can play it professionally, too. And for an extra aesthetic touch, you can purchase this harmonica in a variety of colors.

Fender Blues Deluxe Pros:

- Made by a world-famous guitar and harp manufacturer;
- Beautiful to look at, and;
- Very affordable.

Fender Blues Deluxe Cons:

- Has a very quiet sound, so not a great choice for rock musicians

If you already own a harmonica, check to make sure that it's diatonic. If your harmonica has more than 10 holes, you should purchase one that will be easier to learn on first. Again, all of the instructions and songs in this book are written for 10-hole diatonic harmonicas. It's also advisable to make sure that your harmonica is tuned to the key of C. Remember, diatonic harmonicas can come in any of the 12 keys, but C harmonicas are by far the easiest to learn music theory with. Some harmonicas will have the type and tuning printed on the box, or even the cover plate.

As you begin to improve, you can start to branch out and purchase diatonic harmonicas in different keys. C, A, D, F, and G is the recommended order for beginners. You'll want the key your harmonica is tuned in to match the key that the song you're playing is written in. To learn the basics, all you need is a C harmonica, as you won't be playing songs quite yet.

No matter what key the harmonica is tuned to, the notes are organized the same way. So if you're already familiar with music theory and own a diatonic harmonica tuned to a key other than C, you will have no problem using this book to learn. But if you set out to buy a harmonica, your very first one should always be tuned to C.

Shopping for Harmonicas and Making Your First Sounds

Eagle77. (n.d.). *harmonica blues harp* [Photograph]. Pixabay
https://pixabay.com/photos/harmonica-blues-harp-harp-blues-2812842/

Though there are hundreds of harmonicas available for sale online, you will have the best experience in a local music shop. Unless it specializes in a certain instrument, your local music shop is likely to have at least a few harmonicas for sale. Though there's nothing wrong with shopping online, there are a few advantages to buying your harmonica in person.

First and foremost, you won't have to wait for your harmonica to arrive in the mail to start playing. If you know what you want, you can have a brand new harmonica in a matter of minutes. And the more harmonicas your local shop sells, the more likely they are to order more, increasing the chances of you being able to buy more and better harmonicas from the same shop in the future.

You also don't have to deal with shipping costs, which can sometimes be quite steep if you're purchasing from an international brand. Shipping costs can easily make what should have been an economical purchase into a much pricier investment. Most importantly of all, you can be 100% sure that you're buying a quality instrument. Unlike shopping online, you can physically see and hold a harmonica in a shop before you purchase it. Not only will you be able to chat with someone who is intimately familiar with all of the instruments available for purchase, but you will be able to try out different instruments to determine which one you like best.

If you find a harmonica that you like, you can use the shop's harmonica tester to hear what it sounds like. This ensures that your lips will be the first to touch the instrument's mouthpiece if you decide to make a purchase. The harmonica tester is a special kind of bellow that you push to hear the blow notes and spring back to sound the draw notes. This will help you to hear if all the notes in the harmonica work. If you manage to sound several notes simultaneously, you can also hear whether or not the harmonica is in tune. If you're new to music theory, don't worry—if it sounds bad, it's probably out of tune.

Despite these advantages, it's still possible to make a good harmonica purchase through an online shop. The obvious advantage of shopping online is that you have a much wider selection and can often find good-quality instruments for much lower prices. However, when pricing your instrument online, make sure to factor in the cost of shipping, especially if you're purchasing from an international shop. Always be sure to research the reputation of an online merchant. Make sure that the seller you're buying from has quick and efficient shipping to avoid long waits, or worse, losing your instrument in the mail. Most reputable shops will allow you to see customer reviews. However, you should also check out unaffiliated harmonica discussion groups online to see what other people's experiences have been with the shop you're looking to purchase from (Yerxa, 2016b).

Whether you choose to shop online or in a shop, there are a few things to watch out for. Your first harmonica doesn't have to be top-quality, but it should be airtight and responsive to your breath. This is why the price is such an important indicator. The cheaper the harmonica, the more likely it is to be leaky and unresponsive. Thirty dollars is a very reasonable price for a first harmonica. A little less will still be decent enough to play, and a little more just means that you're getting an instrument that will last you longer. Whatever you do, never go for a harmonica that costs less than $8, and that includes ones that are free. If the instrument is that cheap, it almost certainly means that it's poorly made. However, don't feel pressured to purchase anything upwards of $50. It's actually quite common for first-time players to damage their instrument by blowing too hard, so it's probably not worth it to break the bank on a top-quality instrument. Watch for the brand names Hering, Hohner, Lee Oskar, Seydel, Suzuki, and Tombo. These manufacturers are highly reputable, so you're nearly guaranteed to get a well-made instrument (Yerxa, 2016b).

Once you've purchased your harmonica, it's time to start playing! First, you'll have to become familiar with the notes you can play on your harmonica. Many beginners find themselves a bit confused with the layout of the notes on a harmonica, especially since many musical notes seem to be "missing."

If you've purchased a diatonic harmonica, then it will come pre-tuned to a specific musical key. Most of these harmonicas are tuned to the key of C, and it's that notation that we will be using throughout this book. "Blow" notes are what you hear when you blow into a specific hole, while "draw" notes are what you hear when you suck air in through the same hole.

Almost every harmonica will follow the *Richter Tuning*, making it very easy to switch from one harmonica to the next. For a C harmonica, the tuning will be arranged as follows (Eyers, n.d.):

Hole 4 (Blow) - C

Hole 4 (Draw) - D

Hole 5 (Blow) - E

Hole 5 (Draw) - F

Hole 6 (Blow) - G

Hole 6 (Draw) - A

Hole 7 (Blow) - C

Hole 7 (Draw) - B

Hole 8 (Blow) - E

Hole 8 (Draw) - D

Hole 9 (Blow) - G

Hole 9 (Draw) - F

Hole 10 (Blow) - C

Hole 10 (Draw) - A

Hole 1 (Blow) - C

Hole 1 (Draw) - D

Hole 2 (Blow) - E

Hole 2 (Draw) - G

Hole 3 (Blow) - G

Hole 3 (Draw) - B

This notation begins with hole 4 because that's the hole that's always tuned to the first note in the key. In a C harmonica, the notes in holes 4–7 are C, D, E, F, G, A, B, C, which are the notes in a C major scale. As this is the scale to which a C harmonica is tuned, this makes sense.

The first three holes work a bit differently. Starting with hole 1 and continuing to hole 4, the notes are C, D, E, G, G, B, D, C. This doesn't make up any scale at all. For those who are familiar with music theory, this might seem a bit confusing. But if you look at the blow notes for holes 1–4, you'll see that they are C, E, G, and C. These four notes make up a C major chord. If you blow into the first four holes all at once, you can hear it. Listen to how the notes seem to work in harmony with one another.

The harmonica is not just arranged to follow the notes of the scale—the entire harmonica is arranged in chord groups. The blow notes for holes 4–7 are also C, E, G, and C. This forms yet another C chord, just one octave higher. And the blow notes for holes 7–10? Yes, they are also C, E, G, and C.

The draw notes are also arranged to form playable chords. The draw notes on holes 1–4 are D, G, B, and D, which form the G chord. G chords are very important when playing music in the key of C. To hear how the two chords match each other, try making the chords one after the other. The harmonica is intentionally arranged this way, and this is why the blow and draw notes follow a standardized pattern. The logic behind the Richter tuning is to give you the ability to play both individual notes along a certain scale and the major chords in that key in three different octaves, making the harmonica quite a versatile instrument indeed (Eyers, n.d.).

Playing Notes and Reading Tabs - Getting Started on Your Harmonica

To begin playing notes on your harmonica, you'll want to practice making sounds through simple blowing and drawing. Since each hole makes two different notes, most harmonica notation will refer to the ten holes by their number, rather than by the notes it produces. From holes 1-10, the blow notes on a C harmonica are: C, E, G, C, E, G, C, E, G, C. The draw notes are: D, G, B, D, F, A, B, D, F, A. Using simple blowing and drawing, the harmonica is only capable of producing the seven notes in a C major scale. As such, this is the scale that you will learn first. However, by using bends, it's possible to play all of the notes in a chromatic scale on a diatonic harmonica.

To play a note, use your mouth to find a single hole. Either blow air into the hole or suck air back into it to play a blow note or a draw note. You can do this using one of two techniques with your lips. You can *pucker* your lips around your chosen hole as if you were kissing or whistling. You can also leave your lips relaxed and simply use your tongue to block the three holes to the left of the hole you wish to play through. Either of these techniques is acceptable—the choice depends on what is easiest and most comfortable for you (Yerxa, 2020).

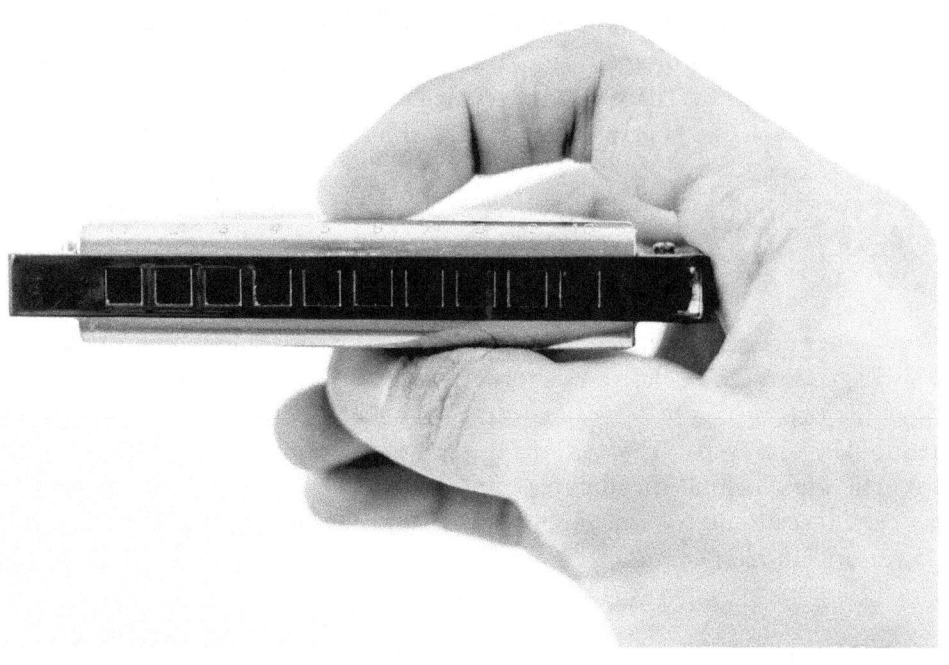

jirawatfoto. (n.d.). *color photo of an old harmonica in hand* [Photograph]. Shuttershock. https://www.shutterstock.com/image-photo/color-photo-old-harmonica-hand-130957787

Holding your harmonica improperly can lead to several problems, including muffled notes and difficulty controlling your harmonica's volume. When holding your harmonica, make sure that it's facing the right way up. The holes of the harmonica should always be facing toward you, with hole 1 on the left and hole 10 on the right. Cup your left hand in a C shape and hold the harmonica between your thumb and index finger. Your forefingers should not cover the hole numbers. Place the middle finger on your left hand behind the harmonica. Place your ring and pinky fingers underneath the harmonica. This cup shape isn't just for stability; the hollow form of your hand will create a resonating chamber for the harmonica's sound. Now place the flat of your right hand over the back of your harmonica, forming a small cup around the instrument. If you're left-handed, follow these instructions in the reverse. This standard position is called a *closed cup*, and is good for lower tones, creating a calming, muted effect. Open your hands slightly when playing higher tones to create a fuller, more resonant sound. Alternating between these two hand positions is how harmonica players achieve a wailing, "wah-wah" effect when they play (Leonhardt, 2020).

A few common mistakes that beginners make when first holding their harmonica are (Leonhardt, 2020):

- Playing with only one hand. Not only does this make you more likely to drop the instrument, but you lose the resonance provided by your cupped hands.
- Trying to look at the harmonica while playing. If it helps, close your eyes while you play. This can be a very difficult advice to follow once you're still learning the location of the holes, but

don't get frustrated. Over time, you'll learn the placement of the holes, and the need to look down at the harmonica will disappear.
- Moving your head instead of the harmonica. When you need to jump from one hole to the next, don't turn your head—slide the harmonica. Turning your head restricts the airflow from your throat, compromising your sound quality and making it much harder to play.
- Not taking proper holding techniques seriously. Proper hand-positioning isn't something players have made up—it really does impact the quality of your play.

The most important thing to remember when you start to play is to *relax*. Resist the urge to huff and puff into your harmonica. Before you bring the instrument up to your lips, take a few deep breaths to steady your breathing patterns. When you breathe, start from your diaphragm. Diaphragm breathing is often easier (and feels more natural) when you breathe through your nose, rather than through your mouth. When you first place the harmonica to your mouth, lick your lips and a few of the middle holes. Bring the harmonica to rest just inside your lips, so the holes sit right in front of your teeth. The deeper you can hold the harmonica inside your mouth while still breathing normally, the better your sound will be. Now drop your lower jaw, take a few deep breaths to get comfortable holding the harmonica in your mouth, and make sure you're sitting up straight, with your shoulders back (Chrapka, 2018b).

You may be relieved to know that you don't have to read music to play the harmonica. In fact, many players prefer to use a kind of notation called *harmonica tablature*, or *harmonica tabs* for short. If you play another instrument, you may already be familiar with tablature as a way to read and write music. Tabs are a very simple way to present the notes required to play a song. They are extremely popular because they're much easier to read than standard musical notation. Tabs indicate which hole to find the note and whether you should blow or draw. For example, "hole 6 draw" refers to the A note in hole 6, and "hole 10 blow" refers to the C note in hole 10 (Chrapka, 2018a). This is often shortened further to "6 draw" or "10 blow." Tabs don't include other musical information, such as rhythm, silence, accents, or dynamics to make it as simple as possible to read. Some harmonica tabs use arrows to indicate more advanced harmonica techniques like bends, but most don't. Tabs simply tell you which holes to play and which note to make on that hole. The only musical information you can glean from this kind of notation is the note and its pitch.

Harmonica tabs will look slightly different depending on the type of harmonica you're using. A diatonic harmonica tab is only designed to indicate the hole (or cell) number, and whether it's a blow or draw note. A tab might look something like this: +5 -4 +3 -2 +1. The numbers indicate which hole to play. A plus sign before a number tells you that note is a blow note, while a minus sign tells you that note is a draw note. So in this tab, "+5" means "5 blow," and "-4" means "4 draw." Be advised that not all harmonica tabs are notated the same way. A few of the more common techniques are:
- **Arrows**. An up arrow means "blow," while a down arrow means "draw." Arrows are particularly common in tabs that use bending techniques, as arrows set at an angle can help to indicate the direction of a bend. Some notations place small, parallel lines above the arrow to indicate a bend. For example, two lines above a down arrow indicate a whole step draw bend. The arrow system is the most versatile, as it allows for much more sophisticated directions.

- **Brackets.** Some tabs put the draw notes in brackets, that look like this: 5 [4] 3 [2] 1. In this kind of notation, a "b" is typically placed next to the hole number to indicate the need for a bend.

Tabs aren't limited to single notes. They can also be used to help you play chords. For example: +4 -5 +3456 -5. In this notation, "+6543" is a chord, asking you to play the blow notes on holes 3–6 all at the same time.

It's as simple as that. If you're already familiar with a certain tune and want to learn how to play, all you have to do is find a harmonica tab and start playing along. This is why tabs are so often recommended to beginning players, even if you already know how to read sheet music. Learning how to play with tabs will help you become familiar with the different parts of the instrument, training your ear to associate the correct notes with the corresponding holes.

However, it's not possible to determine a song's rhythm from a harmonica tab. It will tell you which holes to play the notes on, and that's it. It won't tell you how long to hold those notes or how long to pause in between them. Unless you already know the song or have access to a recording of someone else playing it, it can be very difficult to learn a song from tablature alone. This is the only benefit of learning how to read sheet music. Though it can be difficult and time-consuming, it also gives you the ability to learn any song by simply reading the notation, without having ever heard the song before. Tabs are only useful if you already know the song. Fortunately, "knowing" a song is very easy in the age of the internet. If you can find a recording of the song you want to learn online, you can follow along with your harmonica tabs (*What Are Harmonica Tabs or Harmonica Tablature?*, 2020). Therefore, if you find a song you want to play, first find a way to listen to it. Having the song in your ear will be an important guide to help you correctly navigate the tablature. Without having the song in your head, it will be nearly impossible to play it correctly or confidently.

Harptabs.com is an extremely popular resource for beginning harmonica players, with thousands of songs written out in tabs. However, before you jump in, it's important to learn what notes are possible to play on a C harmonica when you start using bends. Not every single note on the harmonica can be bent, but those that can give you the ability to play more notes. The possible bends on a C harmonica are as follows (Berloto, 2020):

Hole 4 - Db (read "D flat"), half-bend draw

Hole 6 - Ab, half-bend draw

Hole 8 - Eb, half-bend blow

Hole 9 - Gb, half-bend blow

Hole 10 - B, half-bend blow, Bb, whole bend blow

Hole 1 - Db, half-bend draw

Hole 2 - Gb, half-bend draw, F, whole bend draw

Hole 3 - Bb, half-bend draw, A, whole bend draw, Ab, whole and half-bend draw

A "half-bend" simply lowers the note by one half-step, essentially making the note "flat." A "whole bend" lowers the note by one entire step, allowing you to play an entirely new note without changing holes.

For an example of how a harmonica tab might work, let's look at "Ode to Joy" by Beethoven. This song is written in the key of C, and so is compatible with a C harmonica. Read this simple tab from left to right and top to bottom, following along on your harmonica if you know the tune:

+5 -5 +6 +6 -5 +5 -4 +4 +4 -4 +5 +5 -4

+5 -5 +6 +6 -5 +5 -4 +4 +4 -4 +5 -4 +4

-4 +5 +4 -4 +5 -5 +5 +4 -4 +5 -5 +5 -4

+4 -4 +3

+5 -5 +6 +6 -5 +5 -4 +4 +4 -4 +5 -4 +4

Chapter 3:
Techniques for Playing

At this point, you've successfully played your first notes on the harmonica and have perhaps even stumbled your way through your first song. Congratulations! But to continue playing successfully, there are a few basic techniques that you'll need to master.

Embouchure is the position of your lips and tongue when playing a wind instrument. All wind instruments have a variety of embouchures, the harmonica included. Whether you're playing melodies, songs, or solos, different embouchures will slightly change your sound quality. The two basic harmonica embouchures are puckering and tongue blocking. As a beginner, you'll likely start to favor one of these embouchures, but truly skilled players will become adept at both. Even learning just one of these embouchures will greatly improve your play. After you feel comfortable with these two basic embouchures, you can move on to slightly more advanced mouth positions to further improve your skill. Though it is possible to play chords on the harmonica, more often than not, you'll be playing single notes, so that is what you should focus on doing successfully at the beginning.

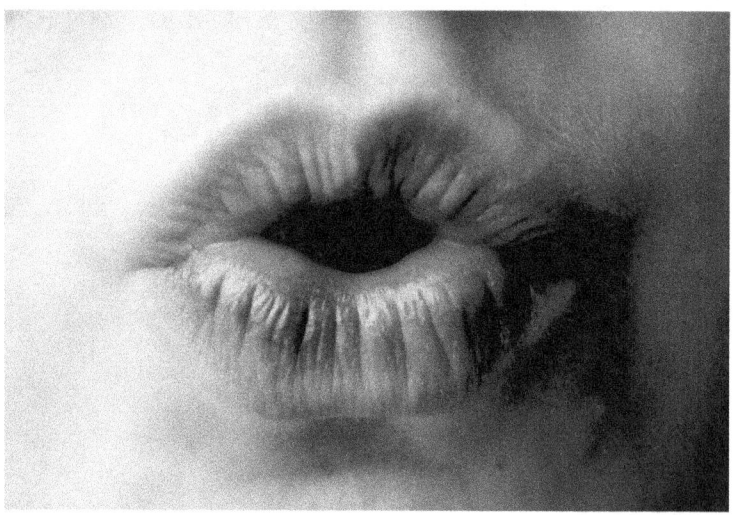

Freeman-Woolpert, J. (n.d.). *lips* [Photograph]. FreeImages. https://www.freeimages.com/photo/lips-1433579

When you pucker, you close your lips around a single hole, as if you're holding a straw in your mouth. The biggest advantage of this technique is that it's extremely easy to learn. It also frees up the tongue, making it possible to learn tongue-based blues techniques in the future. This embouchure is also the preferred method for playing short, staccato notes. However, the disadvantage of relying on this embouchure is that it's very difficult to play in a legato style this way, as you would have to perfect the technique of sliding the entire harmonica very fluidly and gently from side-to-side. This technique also relies very heavily on good breathing techniques and necessitates that airflow is almost entirely regulated through the nose.

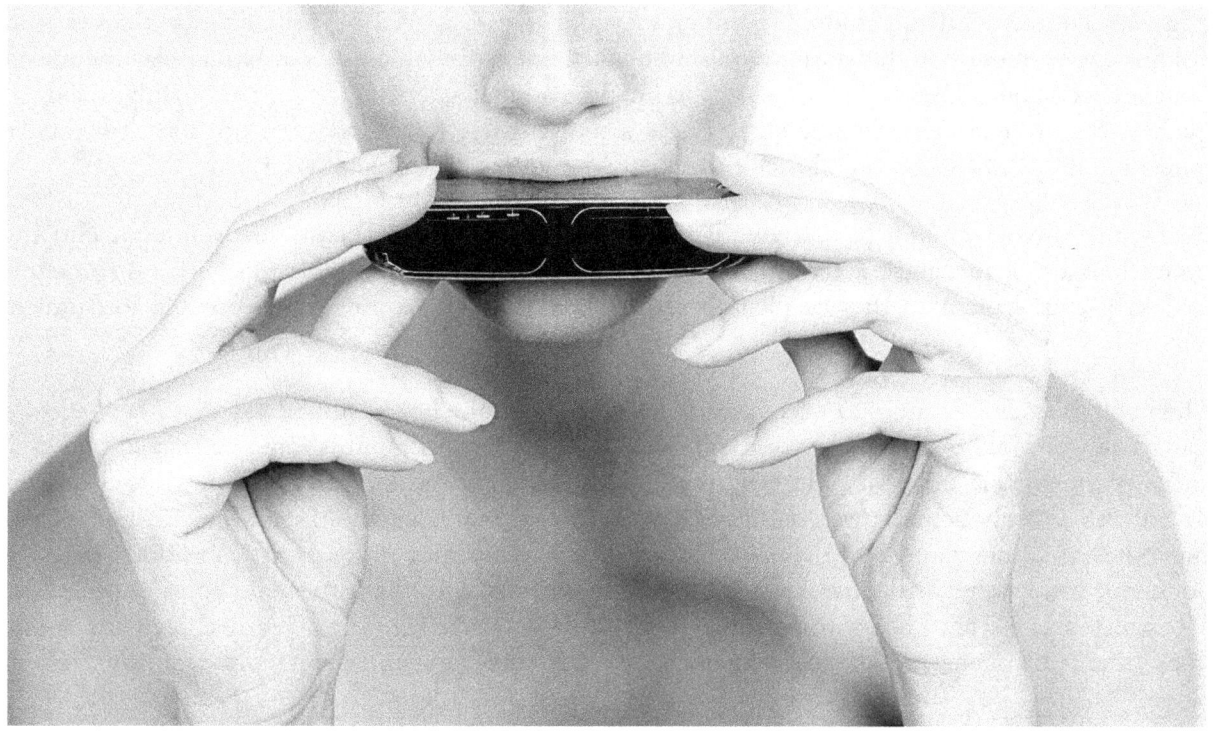

kalcutta. (n.d.). *a beautiful young woman is playing harmonica* [Photograph].
https://www.shutterstock.com/image-photo/beautiful-young-woman-playing-harmonica-close-139414730

Many skilled players prefer the tongue block embouchure, as many genre-specific effects can only be achieved using this method. To use the tongue block, leave your lips open and relaxed. Use your tongue to block the four holes to the left of the hole you wish to play. This will involve stretching your mouth over five holes at once. The fifth hole is the one you're playing, the only hole your lips are covering that isn't blocked by your tongue (Yerxa, 2020). This is a very difficult embouchure to master, especially for beginners, but it's essential if you wish to play jazz or classical music.

To do this technique successfully, allow the harmonica to sit as deep in your mouth as possible while still breathing normally. Tilt the harmonica slightly so that the mouthpiece is at a downward angle. This allows you to use more of your tongue when blocking the holes. Place your tongue on the harmonica first, and then close your lips around it. When playing lower notes, you'll move your tongue to block the four holes to the right of the note you're trying to play. The biggest advantage of this technique is that it greatly increases the volume of your notes, making it a great choice for live players. It also greatly improves your tonal quality while you play and allows you to play for much longer periods without feeling fatigued or winded. However, it is much harder to bend notes using this embouchure. It's also much more difficult to learn tongue-based effects, making this a less reliable embouchure for blues players.

Since blues players use so many tongue-based effects, many of them prefer the lip block embouchure. To use this technique, stretch your mouth over four holes at once. Tilt the harmonica until your lower lip makes contact with the comb. At this point, your upper lip will be resting on the cover plate. Holding the harmonica in this position, play individual notes the same way you would play them using a pucker technique. The difference with this method is that it opens the throat slightly, making it much easier to bend. This technique produces a much softer tone, and so is not ideal for loud or upbeat tunes. It can also be very difficult to achieve a good quality of sound this way.

Finally, the U-block embouchure is a variation on the tongue block. To use this technique, curl your tongue into a U shape, and use the small tunnel it forms to direct air into the holes. This is sometimes used as a complement to the tongue block, for staccato passages or to increase the instrument's volume.

When you're reading harmonica tabs, most will only tell you the hole number and whether to blow or draw. They tell you nothing about your embouchure or how your mouth should be shaped because if you're playing single notes, it ultimately doesn't matter at the beginner level. However, chords are played with an embouchure that's halfway between the tongue block and the pucker method. To play four notes at a time, you'll leave your mouth relaxed over all four notes as if you're doing a tongue block, but you won't actually block any of the holes. However, to make more complex chords, some tabs will indicate which holes you should block with your tongue. If you've mastered the tongue block, then this opens the way for you to easily start practicing these new and interesting chords (Yerxa, 2020).

For example, a tab might look something like this:

+4 -5 +3456 -2XX5

In this case, the two Xs indicate the two holes that should be blocked, allowing you to sound the draw notes for holes two and five simultaneously, forming a chord that is more interesting than a C major chord.

The *position* of the harmonica doesn't indicate what you're doing with your hands—it refers to the relationship between the key that the harmonica is tuned to and the key of the song that you're trying to play. Each position comes with its own sounds and musical possibilities, no matter what key the harmonica is tuned in. The most common harmonica positions are (Yerxa, 2020):

- 1st Position: used for melodies in major keys, songs written to accompany a fiddle, country songs, folk songs, and blues songs.
- 2nd Position: used for melodies in major keys, songs written to accompany a fiddle with a flat 7th, songs written in major keys with notes that fall below the "home" note, or hole 4's blow note, and blues songs.
- 3rd Position: used for melodies in minor keys, songs written to accompany a fiddle, and blues songs written in minor keys.

- 4th Position: used for songs written in minor keys.
- 5th Position: used for songs written in minor keys, but in this position, draw 5 and 6 are still major notes.
- 12th Position: used for songs written in major keys.

Though these are the most common positions, there are 12 harmonica positions in total. The 1st Position is always the key that your harmonica is tuned to (so for a C harmonica, 1st Position is the key of C). Count five scale steps up from the key of the harmonica to reach the next numbered position. So for a C harmonica, 2nd Position is the key of G.

Bending

佐.伯.楽. (n.d.). *harmonica black and white blues* [Photograph]. Pixabay. https://pixabay.com/photos/harmonica-black-and-white-blues-510197/

Understanding the proper way to play the notes on your harmonica is the foundation of harmonica playing. Mastering the two basic embouchures will ensure that you can play individual notes properly and set you well on the path to producing a clear, melodic, and beautiful sound. But learning these two basic positions will also give you the ability to start learning more advanced techniques.

For example, those who wish to play jazz or classical music should master the tongue block. There are many effects and techniques in these genres that require the use of the tongue, including octaves, side-pull, pull, slap, and self-accompaniment. It enables you to play in both legato and staccato style and easily transition between the two. It can be used to increase your volume, which is a useful technique for rock musicians. It can increase your tonal quality, especially when paired with different positions in the throat and mouth. It also allows you to play for longer without getting winded. Learning these effects will be much more difficult if you haven't mastered the basics. Classical harmonica, especially, tends to be more musically complex than other genres So it often calls for specialized chords, playing in positions well above the 1st, and playing notes on the chromatic scale that a diatonic harmonica is not necessarily tuned to play.

However, there is one important technique that is very difficult to achieve using the tongue block, and that's *bending*. This is the main reason why skilled players commit to learning both the pucker and the tongue block, no matter which genre or style they like to play (Chrapka, 2018a). If you're playing a diatonic harmonica, then the only notes that your harmonica is built to play are the seven notes in the scale to which it's tuned. If you include the notes that are repeated up and down the octave, the entire instrument can only play 20 notes. So if you're playing a C harmonica, then the only notes on your harmonica are the seven notes in the C major scale. If you limit yourself to only playing songs written in C major, this is not a problem. But the reality is that music can be written in any of the 12 keys of music. Unless you want to transpose every new song you encounter into C major, you'll have to find a way to play notes that your harmonica was not originally designed to play.

That's where bending comes in. Those who have mastered bending can play any note on the chromatic scale, no matter what key their harmonica is tuned to. This, in turn, makes it possible for them to play any song, written in any key. Bending is what transforms your harmonica from a simple, limited instrument to a fully-fledged "harp," as it's often nicknamed. This is why bending is such an important technique. It's critical for any harmonica player to learn, but it isn't easy to do if you haven't mastered the pucker method of playing notes. Once you've become comfortable playing notes with both of the major embouchures, you're ready to try your hand at bending.

A half-bend pushes the note that you're playing a half-step down. In other words, it makes the note flat. So if the original note is "B," a half-bend would enable you to play Bb (B "flat"). On the other hand, a whole bend pushes the note you're playing up or down an entire step. Not every note on the harmonica is "bendable," but depending on the hole, you can push the note down a half-step, a whole step, or, in the case of hole 1, down a step and a half.

Overblowing or overdrawing is the opposite of bending: depending on the hole, it gives you the ability to raise the note a half step. However, this is quite an advanced technique and should not be attempted until you're comfortable with bending (*The Ultimate Guide to Harmonicas for Curious Newbies*, 2020).

Bending essentially offers two advantages: it allows the player to play more notes, but it also increases the versatility of how you play. If the music requires you to move from one note to the next, you can move the entire harmonica, or you can bend. Bending also enables you to play more notes within one octave. When you're bending a note, you're working with a single reed. So if you're bending the notes in hole 1, for example, the new notes are still going to come out very low, since hole 1 has the biggest reed in the harmonica. You may be able to play the same note without bending, but you won't be able to get it that low.

To successfully bend a note, you'll need to close off your nasal passages and master playing a single note without any air leaking through your lips. The blow notes in holes 8–10 are bendable and are called "blow bends" when they appear in music. The draw notes in holes 1–6 are also bendable and are called "draw bends." To help you practice with draw bends, try covering all of the holes with masking tape, leaving only the hole you're trying to bend exposed.

It's easier to begin with draw 4 to make your first bend. Theoretically, you could start with any of the first six holes, but holes 4 and 6 are the easiest because these bends are very shallow. This means that you don't have to open or close the shape of your mouth to successfully make them happen. In particular, bending hole 1 can be tricky, so don't try to make this your first one. You can practice bending technique without a harmonica, and so if you're having trouble at first, you can try focusing on the shape of your lips and the feeling of the air moving through your throat and mouth. Once you feel comfortable, you can try again with the harmonica at your lips (Yerxa, 2016b).

Before you give bending a try, however, you'll need to do some initial preparation. Make sure that you're comfortable playing regular notes before moving on to this technique. It won't help you to bend if you are still unfamiliar with the basic notes that your harmonica is tuned to play. Before you begin, find an audio recording online of someone playing a harmonica bend on holes 4 and 6 to hear what a bend sounds like. It will be much easier to achieve the right sound if you know what to listen for.

If you're confident playing the basic notes on your harmonica, you're ready to try your first bend. First, find hole 4. Warm yourself up by playing a long, clear draw note. Then play the note again, but as you play, change your tongue's position as if you were making the sound "eee." When you do this, you should hear the note start to sound a little brighter. When you slide your tongue back into its usual "ooh" position, raise it slightly to create a bit of suction. You may hear the note slide down at this point, but if you don't, that's ok! Try making a "kookookoo" with your tongue, lowering your tongue away from the roof of your mouth very slowly and feeling the suction trying to pull your tongue upwards. When you feel the suction, try sliding the flow of air forward and backward along the roof of your mouth. At some point during this process, you'll hear the note slide down, and you'll have made your first bend (Yerxa, 2020).

Bending is not an easy technique to master. You may achieve it on your first day, but it can take days or even weeks of practice to learn for others. Try to be patient with yourself, and don't make bending your only goal. Try practicing and learning other skills while you're trying to master the bend, and with time and patience, it will happen.

Tips and Tricks for Bends, Hand Positions, and Other Playing Techniques

Bending the draw notes in holes 4 and 6 is by far the best place to start when it comes to learning bends. I would recommend beginning with draw 4. Once you're comfortable bending that note, move up to draw 6. Once you feel comfortable bending these notes, you can try bending the draw notes in the lower holes. Draw bends are a good place to start because they're much easier than blow bends.

How exactly do bends work? Believe it or not, no one really knows for sure what the physics is behind harmonica bends. The techniques you'll find in this book and elsewhere come from years of musicians simply experimenting with their instruments, trying to play notes that aren't normally available on their instrument. Bending can be a technique that you use out of necessity (to play new notes that you couldn't play before), but it can also be a stylistic feature, adding a bit of color to your melodies and solos. No matter which note you're playing, bends always have a bit of a dissonant sound, which is why they're so popular in blues and rock music. If you think of your harmonica as a piano, the simple blow and draw notes are the white keys. Bending the notes on your harmonica is like playing the black keys on a piano.

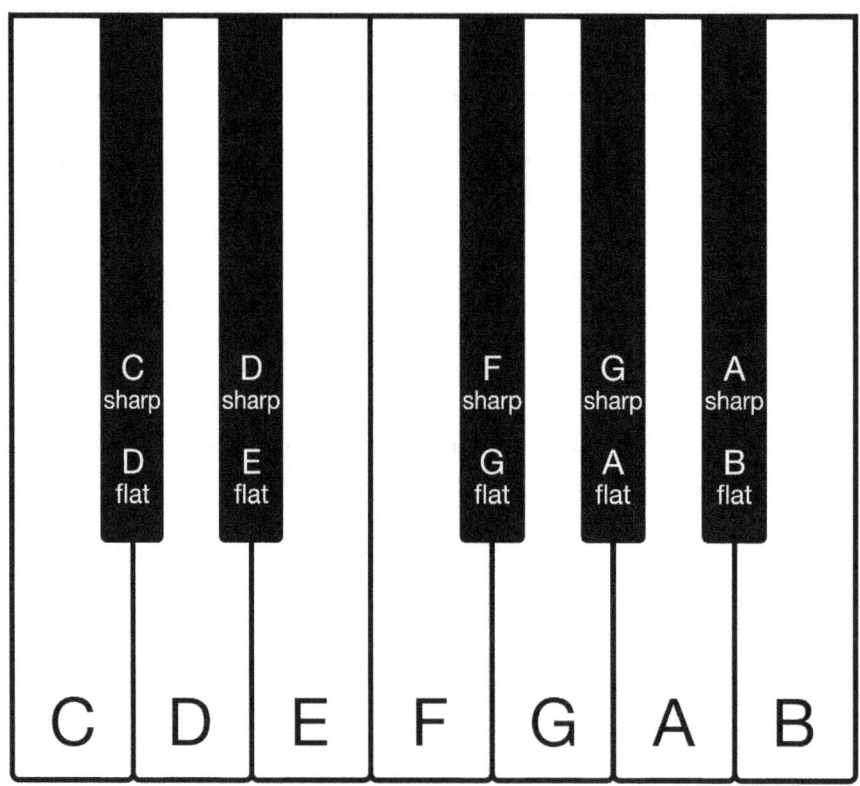

Furian, P. H. (n.d.). *twelve tone chromatic scale on a keyboard* [Photograph]. Shuttershock.
https://www.shutterstock.com/image-vector/twelvetone-chromatic-scale-on-keyboard-one-1439362073

The reason that draw 4 and 6 are the easiest notes to bend is because their reeds are medium-sized. Hole 1 can be difficult to bend because it has such a big reed. And the blow notes at the end of the harmonica all have very small reeds, which are also tricky to manipulate. But by learning to bend draw 4 and 6, you've already added three new notes to your harmonica. Learning the remaining bends will only help you acquire two more (you'll just acquire them in different octaves).

Your first draw bend will be a half-bend, meaning that you're sliding the note down one half-step. In other words, you're making these notes flat. In a chromatic scale, every note is one half-step apart, and in a diatonic scale, every note is a whole step apart. For example, C and Db are a half-step apart.

C and D, on the other hand, are a whole step apart. Bending the draw 4 note (D) will enable you to play the note that is one half-step beneath D, which is Db.

Most draw bends are half-bends. Holes 1, 2, 3, 4, and 6 are bendable, while hole 5 is not. Once you've successfully bent draw 4 and 6, you can move on to draw 3. It's possible to bend this note down three half-steps. The note that draw 3 produces is B, but it can be bent a half-step (Bb), a whole step (A), or a step and a half (Ab). The normal draw note at hole 2 is also A. But learning to bend hole 3 down an entire step will give you an A note that's a little higher in pitch.

As you've already seen, playing draw bends will require you to move both your tongue and the muscles in your throat to direct the flow of air through the harmonica when you inhale. To practice this without a harmonica, try making a whistling sound by inhaling. Now try moving your tongue up and down as you whistle and listen to how the sound changes. This is essentially what's happening when you play a draw bend. If you're struggling to bend, try practicing this way, without the harmonica, for a few days. When you try again with the harmonica in your mouth, you may find the bend a bit more intuitive.

Tips for Draw Bending:

- Use the pucker embouchure. While it's possible to bend using the tongue block method, it's much easier to learn using the pucker method.
- As you draw, lower your tongue and open the back of your throat. If you're having trouble bending, simply practice this to gain better control over the movement of your tongue and throat muscles.
- Resist the urge to draw harder when you're bending. This makes bending more difficult, so try to remain relaxed.
- As you draw, listen to how the note changes when you lower your tongue. If you're familiar with the sound of the note, you'll be able to hear it clearly when the bend is successful.
- Once you've successfully bent the note, try practicing raising it back up by moving your tongue up and down.

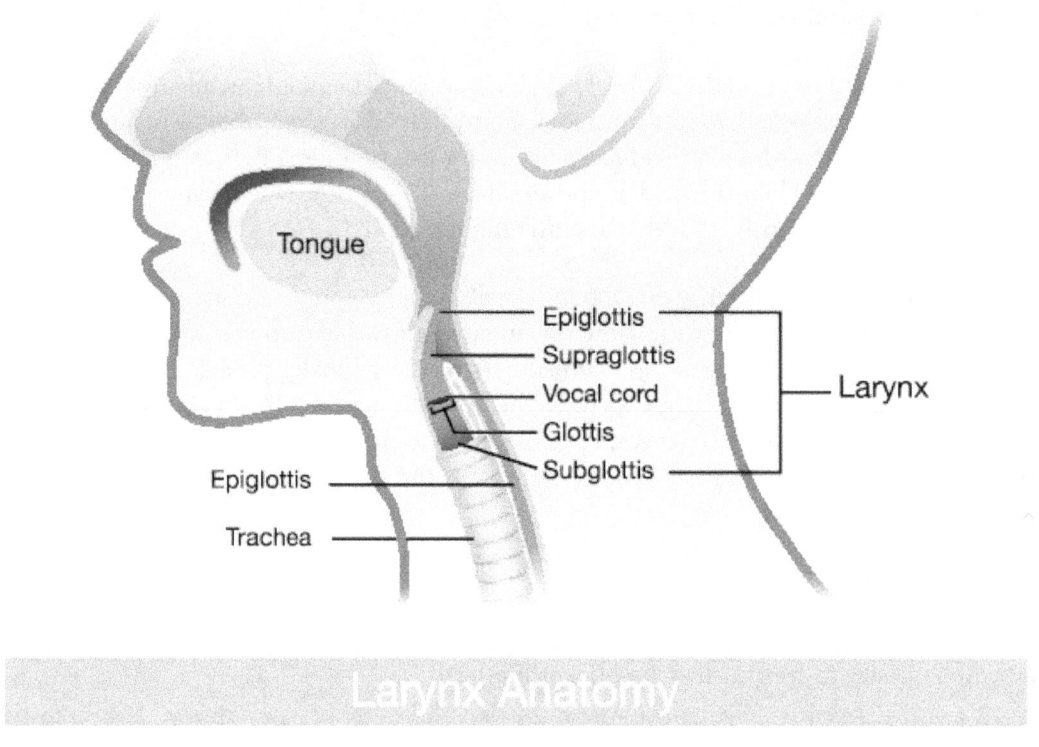

solar22. (n.d.). *human larynx anatomy* [Photograph]. Shuttershock.
https://www.shutterstock.com/image-vector/human-larynx-anatomy-this-illustration-medical-420661489

Draw 4 can be bent using the movement of your tongue alone. Other bends, however (including draw 6), require the correct positioning of your throat. When you open your throat, the muscle that allows that to happen is called the *larynx*. The better control you have over your larynx, the more successful you will be at bending. To practice changing the shape of your larynx, try saying the word "peel" very slowly and feel your throat change position. This is the best position for bending.

Remember that bending is not an easy technique, so don't despair if it takes you a long time to get it right. Each note will require a slightly different movement of your tongue and throat, so expect that some notes will be easier to bend, while others will require more practice to get exactly right. A great way to hear whether your bend was successful is by comparing the bent note to the same note on another instrument, such as a piano or guitar. And, as always, there are plenty of instructional videos online that will let you hear the sound of the bend you're trying to play.

Holes 2 and 3 allow you to bend the notes down three half steps below the normal note. Achieving a whole bend is the same technique as a half-bend; you continue to lower your tongue's position and change the position of your throat. The deeper you lower your tongue, the lower you will be able to bend the note. For example, lower your tongue about halfway down into your mouth to lower draw 2 one half-step (from G to Gb). To lower the note one whole step (from G to F), lower your tongue down into your mouth almost as far as it can go. The more you practice, the better sense you'll get for where your tongue and throat need to be to make the bend successfully.

Musically, blow bends work the same way as draw bends. Blow bends only work on holes 8–10. Just as with draw bends, blow bends lower the blow notes at each of these holes by one half or whole step. They are also similar in technique, in the sense that bends are achieved by changing your tongue's position and your throat muscles to control airflow. However, there are two key differences between blow and draw bending.

First, to blow bend, you move your tongue upward, not downward. Second, rather than opening your throat muscles, you constrict them. This difference is what makes blow bends much more difficult than draw bends. Once you're comfortable with draw bends, the best place to start practicing blow bends is hole 8 (Chrapka, 2018c).

Tips for Blow Bending (8 tips for How to Bend on Harmonica, n.d.):
- **Tilt the harmonica up slightly**. This will make it easier for you to restrict the flow of air into the harmonica as you learn to tighten your throat muscles and close your vocal cords' opening.

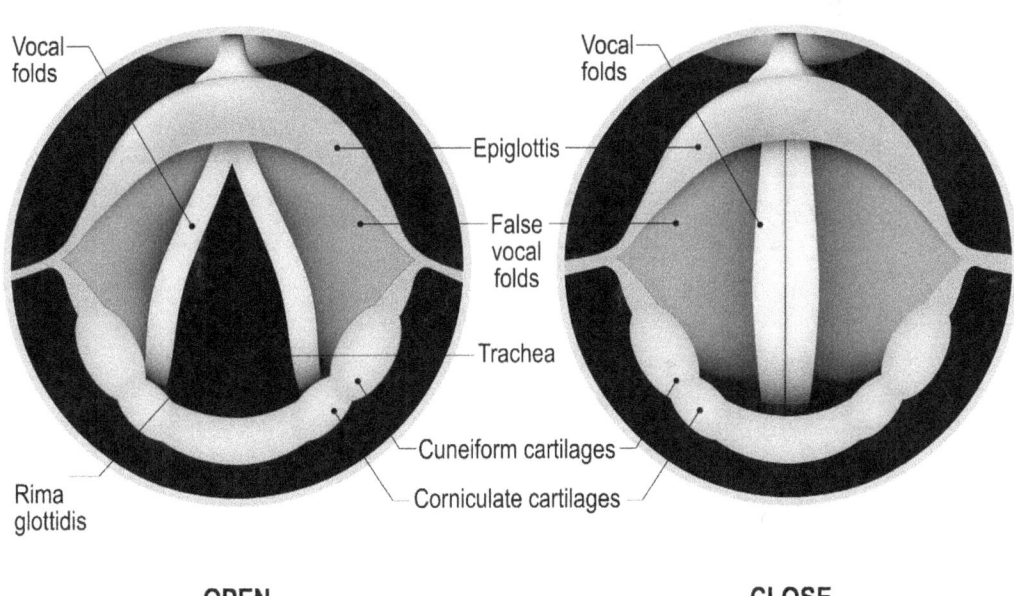

Designua (n.d.). *vocal folds human vocal cords* [Photograph]. Shuttershock. https://www.shutterstock.com/image-vector/vocal-folds-human-voice-cords-open-1098667472

- **Practice making the sounds "eee" and "ooh" with your tongue and throat.** The "eee" position opens your throat, making it easier to draw bend, while the "ooh" position closes your throat, making it easier to blow bend.
- **Train your tongue.** The movements of your tongue should be strong and controlled. If it's flapping around in your mouth too loosely, it won't be easy to control the airflow.
- **Don't pull too far back.** Because you're moving your tongue and thinking about your throat, many beginning players subconsciously pull back from the harmonica. Resist the urge to do this—the deeper the harmonica sits in your mouth, the easier it will be to bend.
- **Don't blow too hard.** It's very common for new players to blow harder than they need to when trying to bend. Not only will this make bending more difficult, but it can damage your harmonica.
- **Don't drop your jaw.** Tightening your throat muscles will cause a slight tightening in your jaw. That's not only very normal but necessary to produce the correct sound.
- **Keep your tongue facing forward.** Once you're comfortable bending with the pucker embouchure, you can try learning how to bend using a tongue block.
- **Keep the harmonica tipped.** When thinking so hard about your tongue and throat, it's easy to forget what you're doing with your hands. Don't allow your hand position to become lazy or the harmonica to sink in your mouth.

chinsoontan. (n.d.). *harmonica folk black and white* [Photograph]. Pixabay. https://pixabay.com/photos/harmonica-folk-black-white-1298900/

And speaking of hand positions, what you do with your hands can actively change the quality of the sound that comes out of your harmonica. Opening and closing your cupped hand around the harmonica can increase or decrease the harmonica's volume. The more open your hands are, the louder the sound, while the tighter you cup your hands around the harmonica, the softer the sound. Closed hands darken the tone of the notes you play, while open hands make the notes much brighter.

It's not only your hands that can change your sound's quality—you can employ your entire arm when playing the harmonica to create slight changes. Using your non-holding hand (this is your left hand for lefties and your right hand for righties), you can "fan" the sound, creating a bright, wavering effect. The further and faster you move your non-holding hand to and away from the harmonica in a fanlike motion, the more dramatic an effect you will produce. You can also rotate your non-holding harm in a half-circle (called the "elbow swing,") or even in a full-circle, to dramatically increase the volume and brighten your sound (Yerxa, 2016c).

Chapter 4:
Playing in Different Positions

809499. (n.d.). *musical instrument mouth organ* [Photograph]. Pixabay.
https://pixabay.com/photos/musical-instrument-mouth-organ-music-653895/

Remember, the "position" of the harmonica speaks to the relationship between the key that the harmonica is tuned to and the key of the music you're trying to play. Positions are numbered and determined in the same way, no matter what kind of harmonica you're playing (Yerxa, 2020).

A position, therefore, is not a fixed musical scale. You can play a blues scale, for example, in multiple positions. Essentially, the position tells you which hole the scale starts from, giving you access to a new key. The key your harmonica is tuned to begins with blow 4. So in a C harmonica, blow 4 produces the note C.

But for those of you who are new to music theory, you have probably been wondering—what exactly *is* a key?

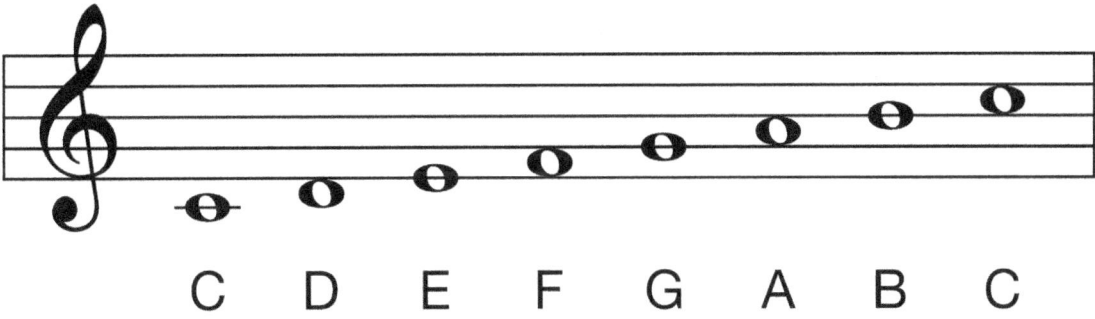

Furian, P. H. (n.d.). *C major scale full notes* [Photograph]. Shuttershock. https://www.shutterstock.com/image-vector/c-major-scale-full-notes-key-1443458357

Essentially, a key is a root note and chord around which everything in the music is structured. So in the key of C, the root note is C, and the root chord is C major. When you play music in the key of C, the music will feel like it somehow resolved itself whenever you play a C note.

The key also tells a musician which notes are most likely to appear in the melody and chords. For example, in music written in the key of C, we can expect to hear the notes C, D, E, F, G, A, B, but in music written in the key of A, we would expect to hear the notes A, B, Db, D, E, Gb, and Ab. The relationship between the root note and the rest of the notes is the same, no matter which key you're working with. For example, the musical distance between C and G is the same as the musical distance between A and E, or five whole steps. This is what we call a "fifth."

It's possible to play the same song in two different keys. The melody of the song will be recognizable, but the pitch will change with the key. If you're a beginning player, then your harmonica is most likely tuned to the key of C. This doesn't mean that you are limited to music that's written in this key, but it does mean that, if you want to play something in a different key, you'll have to change position.

1st Position (Straight Harp)

First position is the key in which your harp is already tuned. For example, if you have an A harmonica, 1st position is the key of A. This root note will be found at blow 4, blow 7, blow 10, and blow 1. First position always starts at blow 4.

2nd Position (Cross Harp)

A great deal of blues harmonica is actually written to be played in 2nd position. This position always starts at draw 2. The root note can be found again at blow 6. So if you have an A harmonica, you will be playing in the key of E if you're in 2nd position. In this position, the notes are typically arranged so that you have easy and natural access to bent notes, which is why so many blues songs are played in this position.

To determine what key 2nd position will be for you, simply count up five whole steps from the root note of your harmonica. So for a C harmonica, 2nd position will be in the key of G. As a beginning player, it's easier to begin with music written in C, as that will help you to become more comfortable with the notes as they are laid out in your harmonica. But the most comfortable next step will be to seek out music written in the key of G, as this music will both sound natural and be very easy to play on your C harmonica. However, music written in any key is theoretically playable on your harmonica. It will just be slightly more difficult the further the musical key is from the key your harmonica is tuned to.

3rd Position (Slant Harp)

Third Position is the most commonly used position when you want to play music written in a minor key. You can certainly play music written in major keys in this position, too, but it's extremely easy to access minor notes and chords in 3rd position. This is because, the way that the notes fall, your regular draw 5 is a perfect minor 3rd.

Third Position starts on draw 4. The root note can be found again on draw 1. Since its sound is so distinctive, it's very easy to determine which key your 3rd position is in. And if you're still new to music theory, count up one whole step from the key in which your harmonica is tuned. So if you have an A harmonica, then 3rd position is B. If you have a C harmonica, 3rd position is D.

But why go through all the trouble of changing positions? Why not just play in the key your harmonica is tuned to?

First and foremost, changing positions is an easy way to access new musical keys, which opens up a huge variety of potential songs that you can play. It also allows you to play musical scales beyond the standard major scale. For example, if you wanted to play a blues scale written in the key of C, you would actually want to use an F harmonica.

Each position is located a full fifth up from the previous position. For example, on a C harmonica, 1st position is C, 2nd position is G, 3rd position is D, 4th position is A, 5th position is E, etc. Positions beyond the 5th are rare, and most harmonica players typically stick to positions 1, 2, and 4.

When you're first starting out, it's easier to learn the key that your harmonica is tuned to first. If you have a C harmonica, start out by learning the key of C. Familiarize yourself with the notes in that key, and where those notes fall on your harmonica. Over time, you'll train your ear to associate the sound with the corresponding note. This will make it easy to bend, but it will also make it much easier to branch out into different keys. The notes don't change. A new key changes the way that the notes are laid out on the harmonica itself.

This is also why it's much easier to start learning to play on a diatonic harmonica, rather than a chromatic one. Diatonic scales are major scales, which means that each note is a whole step above the next. The 10 hole layout in diatonic harmonicas makes it very easy for you to find where the notes are located, and subsequently, makes it easier to change keys. On the other hand, a chromatic scale will include *all* the possible notes in a musical key, including all of the half-steps. Learning to achieve these half-steps on a diatonic harmonica will make switching up to a chromatic harmonica much simpler.

Positions and Modes on a Diatonic C Harmonica

Yummymoon. (n.d.). *harmonica music book* [Photograph]. Pixabay.
https://pixabay.com/photos/harmonica-music-book-wood-621257/

As a beginner, you're most likely learning on a diatonic C harmonica. As such, when learning the different positions, you'll want to understand how they work if 1st position is in the key of C.

If you're feeling a little overwhelmed, don't worry. Harmonica positions and choosing the right key is the most difficult part of harmonica theory. Once you get to a point where you're comfortable changing positions, there will be very little music that you can't play.

The more commonly used positions have nicknames that are also helpful to learn, especially if you plan to interact with other harmonica players or read harmonica blogs. Playing in first position is often called "straight harp" or "playing straight." Second position is often referred to as "cross harp," especially in blues circles (Derhgawen, n.d.).

Think of the positions as different musical scales. Since diatonic harmonicas can come tuned in any key, it's extremely useful to think of changing "position" as simply changing one musical scale for another. The note layout from key to key remains relatively the same. Once you learn a song in a certain key, you can very easily play that song in any key you wish using the same holes.

Learning the position makes communicating and exchanging music with other harmonica players extremely easy. This method of changing scales, however, is relatively unique to the harmonica. If you talk about "changing position" to a guitar or piano player, they'll have no idea what you're trying to say.

To refresh, let's take another look at the note layout on a diatonic C harmonica:

Hole 1 - +(Blow) C, - (Draw) D

Hole 2 - +E, -G

Hole 3 - +G, -B

Hole 4 - +C, -D

Hole 5 - +E, -F

Hole 6 - +G, -A

Hole 7 - +C, -B

Hole 8 - +E, -D

Hole 9 - +G, -F

Hole 10 - +C, -A

The lowest note is blow 1, or C. This is also the root note, the note around which the entire key is built. This is why we call this kind of harmonica a "C" harmonica.

If you're using a new harmonica and you're not sure what key it's in, there are a few easy ways to determine it. For example, imagine you pick up a harmonica in which the notes are laid out like this:

Hole 1 - +G, -B

Hole 2 - +C, -D

Hole 3 - +E, -G

Hole 4 - +G, -B

Hole 5 - +C, -D

Hole 6 - +E, -F

Hole 7 - +G, -A

Hole 8 - +C, -B

Hole 9 - +E, -D

Hole 10 - +G, -F

On this harmonica, the notes that would normally be assigned to hole 1 are found on hole 2. Hole 1, on the other hand, has two entirely new notes. This is a fairly common harmonica notation. Blow 4 is tuned to G, so does that make this a "G" harmonica? Since the blow chord is still C major, and the notes are the notes of the C major scale, we would still call this a "C" harmonica. The change in notes makes very little difference how you play (Derhgawen, n.d.).

Learning to change positions will make it possible for you to play music that isn't written in C major. There are 12 musical keys, and so there are 12 corresponding harmonica positions. On a C harmonica, playing in 1st position means that the musical scale begins and ends with C. The root note can be found at blow 4, blow 7, and blow 1. The note C is the focal center of the music, the tone around which the music is built. Changing positions means changing the placement of the root note. For example, to play in 2nd position (or the key of G), all of the scales would shift slightly, so that they begin and end on the note G. The root chord would now be the G chord, which consists of draw notes 1, 2, 3, and 4.

Shifting to 2nd position means thinking of G as the new root note. As you change positions, you're simply changing the root note to use a new scale and subsequently creating a new play mode. On a C harmonica, 1st position is in the key of C. Second position shifts you to the key of G, 3rd position is the key of D, and 4th position is the key of A. Positions beyond the 4th position are rare. Once you've gotten the hang of changing positions, it becomes easier to play in keys further away from the key of C.

A Closer Look at 1st Position

Otherwise known as "straight harp," this is what happens when you play music in the key of C on your C harmonica. Folk and ragtime players are most likely to use 1st position. To hear 1st position playing at its best, research recordings of Gwen Foster's music online from the 1920s and 1930s. These recordings are worth listening to for all harmonica players, as they demonstrate the great range of sound that a "basic" harmonica can achieve. Other influential 1st position players to listen to are Rhythm Willie and Jimmy Reed.

A Closer Look at 2nd Position

In this position, the harmonica is played a perfect fifth (or five whole steps) above its pre-tuned key. For a C harmonica, this position puts you in the key of G, which is most often used by blues and rock players. Playing in this position mostly makes use of the Draw notes in holes 1–5. Henry Whitter was the first person ever to be recorded playing in cross harp. He wasborn in 1892, and his recording of the "Rain Crow Bill Blues" in 1923 is perhaps his most famous song performed in 2nd position (Derghawen, n.d.).

A Closer Look at 3rd Position

On a C harmonica, 3rd position brings you to the key of D. This brings you to one whole step above the key your harmonica is tuned to. Little Walter is one of the most influential "slant," or 3rd position, players. He became the first player in history to be recorded playing slant when he was featured on Muddy Waters's song, "Lonesome Day" in December, 1951 (Derhgawen, n.d.).

Because this key puts you one whole step above the pre-tuned note, the root note can be found at draw 4. Playing in this position makes use of the draw notes in holes 4–6. Third position always has a very moody sound to it, so it is favored by players who like minor chords. As such, this position is most often used by folk and blues players.

A Closer Look at 4th Position

On a C harmonica, 4th position is in the key of A. Fourth position also has a minor sound, and it is most commonly used for playing minor chords. In 4th position, the root note is draw 3 bent down one whole step. This makes 4th position quite challenging to play so it's not as common as the first three positions.

When and Why to Change Position

Stafford, N. (n.d.). *macro mouth organ* [Photograph] *Pixabay.* https://pixabay.com/photos/macro-mouth-organ-harmonica-5154177/

Different positions lend a slightly different quality to the sound of your harmonica. This is why different positions tend to be favored by musicians in different genres. Because of its bright and clean quality, First position is favored by pop and folk players. On the other hand, 2nd position is most often used by blues and rock players. Third position appears most often in folk and blues songs.

It's still worth it to learn how to play different positions on differently tuned harmonicas. Different keys gain different tonal qualities when played on variously tuned harps. For example, think about your C harmonica. If you wanted to play a blues song in the key of C, you'd be playing in 1st position. On the surface, this would seem to make the most sense. It would certainly be easier to play in 1st position. However, many seasoned players prefer to play the blues in 2nd position. In that case, it would make more sense to play this song on an F harp, where the key of C is 2nd position.

Why do blues players prefer 2nd position over 1st? The draw notes in holes 1–4 are the most bendable, and in 2nd position, you can take advantage of those notes. You can most certainly play the blues in 1st position, or any position, for that matter. But bending the notes in 2nd position gives the melody a distinct tonal quality, one that has come to be deeply associated by audiences with blues music. The same is true for all positions. Each one has distinct tones, styles, and advantages, so the more comfortable you become with them, the better quality music you'll be able to make (*Understanding 1st/2nd position: Two Basic Styles of Playing*, 2019).

A Note on Overbending

As you now know, your diatonic harmonica is designed to play notes in a diatonic scale. In other words, it's only tuned to play the whole notes in any major or minor scale. The only place in the harmonica where a complete scale can be played is in the second octave. Bending enables you to replace some of the "missing" notes, expanding your musical ability. However, bending alone won't give you access to all 12 notes on a chromatic scale, making it impossible to play certain songs.

This is where the technique of overblowing and overdrawing becomes useful. These techniques are the last you need to learn to truly access all of the notes in a complete chromatic scale on a diatonic harmonica. The first overblow ever recorded was made by Blues Birdhead (James Simon) in the 1929 recording of his song, "Mean Low Blues." However, it would be Howard Levy, who would ultimately perfect the technique. Overblowing opened up an entirely new world of possibilities for the diatonic harmonica, which previously had been perceived as humble and ultimately inferior to the chromatic harmonica (Derhgawen, n.d.). It becomes possible to play all 12 positions in all 12 keys on one single diatonic harmonica using overbends. If you don't believe me, listen to the works of Otavio Castro, who plays exclusively on a C diatonic harmonica in all 12 musical keys!

When beginner players first hear the terms "overblow" and "overdraw," they make the mistake of believing that they have to breathe harder to achieve the technique successfully. But as with regular bending, the opposite is true. More importantly, blowing or drawing too forcefully can damage your instrument. Like bending, overbending requires the proper embouchure, control of your tongue and throat muscles, and a great deal of practice. These techniques are intermediate, but understanding the possibilities they open up will help you make better decisions about your harmonica playing in the future.

A Note on Tuning

Like all instruments, diatonic harmonicas can be tuned in an infinite number of ways. The standard tuning is called the Richter tuning, and this method is used for just about any harmonica you purchase. Most harmonica songs and instruction manuals (including this one) are written under the assumption that your harmonica uses this tuning. However, just because it's the most common tuning doesn't mean it's the only possibility. There are many alternate tunings that can make playing in certain styles (especially Irish and Country) much easier.

Country Tuning

A country tuning follows the traditional Richter set-up with Draw 5 raised a half-step. On a normal C harmonica, the regular note on Draw 5 is F. However, on a C harmonica with a country tuning, the regular note on Draw 5 is a Gb. This allows the player to achieve a Gb without overblowing and makes it possible to play a major 7th chord. This is an extremely popular chord progression in country music, so this tuning is popular with country musicians. In 2nd position, this tuning becomes even more versatile. Using a simple draw bend, you can achieve a regular F note on this hole as well.

Natural Minor

This tuning arranges the notes on the harmonica like this:

Hole 1 - +C, -D

Hole 2 - +Eb, -G

Hole 3 - +G, -Bb

Hole 4 - +C, -D

Hole 5 - +Eb, -F

Hole 6 - +G, -A

Hole 7 - +C, -Bb

Hole 8 - +Eb, -D

Hole 9 - +G, -F

Hole 10 - +C, -A

This tuning transforms the blow and draw chords from major chords (as they are normally) to minor chords. Using this tuning makes it much easier to play music written in minor keys (Derhgawen, n.d.).

Diminished Tuning

This tuning arranges the note layout like this:

Hole 1 - +Eb, -F

Hole 2 - +Gb, -Ab

Hole 3 - +A, -B

Hole 4 - +C, -D

Hole 5 - +Eb, -F

Hole 6 - +Gb, -Ab

Hole 7 - +A, -B

Hole 8 - +C, -D

Hole 9 - +Eb, -F

Hole 10 - +Gb, -Ab

This tuning makes it possible to play a complete chromatic scale with the help of simple bending alone. This tuning makes the harmonica extremely versatile musically, and there are possible bends on all 10 holes. This tuning makes it extremely easy to play music in all 12 keys with just one diatonic harmonica. Your harmonica has the same musical versatility as a chromatic harmonica when you use this tuning. However, this is not a friendly tuning to learn on. Mastering precise bending technique is critical before attempting to play in this tuning.

These are only a few of the many possibilities for harmonica tunings. For a nearly complete list of tunings, you can purchase the publication *Altered States* by Pat Missin. You can also download this catalog for free at patmission.com and even purchase a few harmonicas from Lee Oskar with unusual tunings. Hohner offers a similar range of alternate tuning options for their diatonic harmonicas. If you'd like to experiment with special tunings in the future, purchasing a specially tuned harmonica can make branching out much easier and relieve you of the pressure of learning to tune your harmonica yourself (Derhgawan, n.d.). If you wish, it's also possible to purchase diatonic harmonicas tuned to any of the 12 musical keys: G, Ab, A, Bb, B, C, Db, D, Eb, E, F, and Gb.

No matter what tuning your harmonica begins with, remember that it's possible to play a song in any key by simply changing its position. There are several charts available online that you can use to determine which notes make up which keys. When first starting out, it's best to first familiarize yourself with the notes in the C major scale. Once you're comfortable with these notes, you can start bending, which, in turn, will teach you how to listen for additional notes on the chromatic scale (Derghawan, n.d.).

Chapter 5:
Your Musical Style

Hurley, S. (n.d.). *harmonica tambourine and ukulele* [Photograph]. Burst.
https://burst.shopify.com/photos/harmonica-tambourine-and-ukulele?q=harmonica

The harmonica is an extremely versatile instrument, commonly appearing in music across various genres and styles. The most common styles that feature harmonicas are classical, jazz, bluegrass, blues, rock, country, folk, and Celtic. Classical music is the most musically complex genre in which the harmonica (or any instrument) appears. If you wish to play classical harmonica, you will almost certainly need to learn how to read sheet music. Other genres are much more flexible in bringing your own unique style of play to the music. Old-time is particularly accessible to beginners, as it's primarily played in 1st position.

Classical

Diatonic harmonicas are rarely used in classical music, as the music necessitates the ability to play all of the notes on a chromatic scale easily. If you want to play classical harmonica, you will almost certainly have to graduate to a chromatic, chord, polyphonia, bass, or horn harmonica in the future. Each of these specialized harmonicas allows the player to do some extremely advanced musical techniques. Classical pieces are rarely written in tabs, as they are typically too complex and require additional musical information to be played correctly.

Jazz

Jazz harmonica is a bit less technically demanding than classical. Jazz players can play happily and easily on diatonic harmonicas alone, but mastering both bending and overbending is critical if you want to become a jazz musician.

In jazz music, you will rarely find yourself playing alone as a harmonica player. Instead, most jazz pieces will be written to be accompanied by guitar, piano, bass, drums, or various other instruments. In jazz music, harmonicas can take on many different roles, including the main melody, accompaniments, riffs, or even chords (*Harmonica/Music style*, n.d.).

Like classical music, jazz music requires the ability to play all of the notes in a chromatic scale. For this reason, many jazz musicians ultimately upgrade to a chromatic harmonica, simply for ease of play. However, many professional jazz musicians have enjoyed long careers with diatonic harmonicas. The choice will ultimately come down to how technically complex the music you're playing is and how your harmonica plays within that music. If your role is mainly accompaniment, then a diatonic harmonica should be more than sufficient. However, if you are playing main chords or melodies, you may want to consider learning with a chromatic harmonica in the future.

That being said, there is no jazz song that can't be played using bends and overbends. Jazz is a horn-based genre, and so the most common keys jazz music is composed in are Bb, Eb, and Ab. This would mean becoming very familiar with the 3rd, 4th, and 5th positions on a C harmonica. If you are still uncomfortable with overbending, you may want to consider purchasing a Bb, Eb, or Ab diatonic harmonica. You would still need to master overbending eventually, but it would enable you to play most jazz compositions in a comfortable 1st position while you're learning.

Bluegrass

The traditional instruments found in bluegrass music are fiddle, banjo, acoustic guitar, resonator guitar, mandolin, and upright bass. When it appears in bluegrass music, the harmonica is often used as a replacement for the fiddle. Bluegrass music often seems accessible to beginners because players most often use C diatonic harmonicas. However, since you're most likely playing music originally written for the fiddle, you will need to learn how to overbend.

Bluegrass music is much more musically complex than it sounds. This is especially so for harmonica players because you'll need the skill and ability required to play chromatically to replace the fiddle. Fast bluegrass pieces can quickly turn into a lot of huffing and puffing for the unskilled player. More often than not, harmonica appears in bluegrass as a slow, wistful instrument that adds a haunting quality to the music.

Bluegrass purists don't always welcome harmonica, so be mindful of this if you wish to enter the scene. The genre is extremely fiddle-oriented, so to become a bluegrass player, you'll have to train yourself to get to the point where you can compete musically with a fiddle. Many aspiring bluegrass harmonica players pick up the fiddle or banjo and then slowly introduce the harmonica into music scenes where they are already known and respected as a bluegrass musician. An acoustic guitar is a great second instrument to learn, as its musical abilities extend well beyond bluegrass (*Harmonica/Music style*, n.d.).

When learning bluegrass on your own time, start with slower-paced songs. These are the songs that typically feature harmonica anyway, and they are much easier to learn. Once you're comfortable playing slower songs, you can work your way up to faster-paced pieces. If you wish to enter the bluegrass music scenes as a musician, it may be best to learn the same song on the harmonica, the fiddle, or the banjo. That way, you have more options, and are less likely to get bounced out of the scene by purists.

Bluegrass is an extremely precise music scene. Like classical music, effects like blues notes or wails are rarely welcome and are never intentionally written into the music. If you're serious about learning bluegrass, this may be a good thing, as you won't necessarily need to learn any fancy effects or genre-specific techniques to be a proficient player. It's helpful to listen to a saxophone or a trumpet playing the two different genres to understand the stylistic differences between bluegrass and blues. A bluegrass saxophone will sound much more precise and polished than a blues saxophone, which will sound more, well, bluesy. The same is true for the harmonica.

Since bluegrass is played chromatically, many bluegrass players acquire two or three diatonic harmonicas, each tuned to a different key. If you're really serious about bluegrass, you may even want to consider upgrading to a C chromatic harmonica in the future.

Blues, Rock, and Country

In all three of these genres, the traditional instruments are vocals, bass, percussion (usually a drum set), and guitar. In blues and country, the harmonica is also considered a "traditional" instrument, making these the most popular starting genres for budding harmonica players. These genres are typically the most fun to play, as the harmonica often carries some of the main melodies.

In blues music, it's very common to use a diatonic harmonica in the 2nd position. However, if you've mastered basic bending, you can play most music in any of these genres, regardless of the key it's written in. Blues, in particular, makes a great deal of use out of bends, to the point that playing another kind of harmonica can actually make it more difficult to get a true blues sound.

Blues purists will insist on playing exclusively in the 2nd position, and subsequently tend to collect harmonicas in various keys to make this possible at all times. On the other hand, rock and country are far less rigid in terms of genre traditions or norms. All three of these genres make far more use of chords than bluegrass, jazz, or classical. Blues music, in particular, is most often written in the following keys: G, A, Bb, C, D, E, and F. If you're using a C harmonica, this means becoming comfortable with the 1st, 2nd, 3rd, 4th, 5th, 11th, and 12th positions. Alternatively, you may want to consider purchasing a G or A harmonica in the future. This will make switching keys much easier and give you access to three possible 2nd Positions (*Harmonica/Music style,* n.d.).

Across all three of these genres, however, the most common keys used are A, C, D, and F. On a C harmonica, this would be the 1st, 3rd, 4th, and 12th positions. Purchasing an A or a D harmonica would enable you to play almost any song in all three genres in just 1st or 2nd position. Harmonicas are particularly common in blues because it's the harmonica preferred by Little Walter, one of the most influential blues harmonica players. And, of course, to play songs in the key of A in 2nd position, you may want to consider purchasing a D harmonica. F harmonicas are also popular choices for blues players, as this enables you to play C music in 2nd position.

Harmonica Tabs for Classic Rock

At this point, you've mastered the basic playing technique on the C harmonica. Now it's time to play! Though there are thousands of free tabs available online, here are a few tabs for classic rock songs to get you playing popular tunes in a fun and accessible genre. Notes without a minus sign should be played as blow notes, while a < indicates a half-bend, and a << indicates a whole bend. Notes in parentheses indicate that the two notes should be played at the same time to form a chord (*Today's 20 Most Popular Songs,* n.d.):

Piano Man - Billy Joel

Key: C

6 -6 6 -5 5 -5 5

4 -4 5 -4

5 -5 6 -6 6 -5 5 -5 5

4 -5 5 -4 4

Making love to his tonic and gin

5 -5 6 -6 6 -5 5 -5 5

4 -5 5 -4 5

-4 5 -5

You've got us feeling alright

5 -5 6 -6 6 -5 5 -5 5

4 -5 5 -4 5

And probably will be for life

5 -5 6 -6 6 -5 5 -5 5

4 -5 5 -4 5

Piano solo

-4 5 -5

You've got us feeling alright

5 -5 6 -6 6 -5 5 -5 5

4 -5 5 -4 5

-4 5 -5

You've got us feeling alright

5 -5 6 -6 6 -5 5 -5 5

4 -5 5 -4 5

We Are the Champions - Queen

Key: C

3 3 4 4 3 -3 -3 4

I've paid my dues, time after time

3 3 -3 4 4 3 3 -4 4 -3 4

I've done my sentence, but committed no crime

4 4 -5 -5 4 5 -5 -5

And bad mistakes, I've made a few

4 4 5 -5 -5 -5 6 -5 6 -6

I've had my share of sand kicked in my face

-6 -7 -6 -7 7

But I've come through

7 -7 7 -7 6 5 -6 5

We are the champions, my friends

6 7 -8 8 9 8 -6 -7 -6

And we'll keep on fighting till the end

-6 6 -6 6 -5 8 -8 8 -8 7

We are the champions, we are the champions

8 -8 8 -8 7

No time for losers

-6 8 -8 8 -8 7 -6 6 7

'Cause we are the champions, of the world

3 3 -3 -3 4 3 3 -3 -4 4

I've taken my bows, and my curtain calls

3 3 3 4 4 4 4

You brought me fame and fortune

4 4 4 -4 -4 -4 4 -3

and everything that goes with it

3 -3 -4 4

I thank you all

4 4 4 5 5 5 -5 -5

But it's been no bed of roses

4 4 -5 -5 -5 -5 -5 -5 -5-5 6 6

No pleasure cruise, I consider it a challenge

6 6 6 -6 -6 -6 -7 -7 -7 -7 -6 -7 7

before the whole human race and I ain't gonna lose

7 -7 7 -7 6 5 -6 5

We are the champions, my friends

6 7 -8 8 9 8 -6 -7 -6

And we'll keep on fighting, till the end

-6 6 -6 6 -5 8 -8 8 -8 7

We are the champions, we are the champions

8 -8 8 -8 7

No time for losers

-6 8 -8 8 -8 7 -6 6 7

'Cause we are the champions, of the world

Midnight Rambler - Rolling Stones

Key: E

-3 -(3 4) -2 -2 b-2 -2

-3 -(3 4) -2 -2 b-2 -2

<-2 -2 -(2 3) -(2 3) -(2 3)

Did ya hear about the midnight rambler

<-2 -(23)-(23)

Everybody got to go

<-2 -2 -(23) -(23) -(23)

Did you hear about the midnight rambler

<-2 -2 -2 -2

The one that shut the kitchen door

<-2 -2 -(23) -(23)

Don`t give no hoot 'bout warning

<-2 -2-(23)-(23)-(23)

Wrapped up in a blackjack cloak

<-2 -2-(23)-(23)-(23)

He don`t go in the light of morning

<-2-2-2-(23)-(23)

Worried that the cock'll crow

<-2 -2 -2 -2

<-1 -1 -(12)-(12) <-1 -1 -(12) -(12) -(23) -(23)

<-1 -1 -(23)-(23) <-1 -1 -(23) -(23) <-1 -1 -(23)

Talk about the midnight gambler

Hey Jude - The Beatles

Key: C

6 5 5 6 -6 -4 -4 5 -5 7 7 -7 6 -6 6 -5 5

Hey, Jude, don't make it bad; take a sad song and make it better

6 -6 -6 -6 -8 7 -7 7 -6 6 4 -4 5 -6 6 6 -5 5 -3

4 4

Remember to let her into your heart, then you can start to make it

better.

6 5 5 6 -6 -4 -4 5 -5 7 7 -7 6 6 6 -5 5

Hey, Jude, don't be afraid, you were made to go out and get her.

6 -6 -6 -6 -8 7 -7 7 -6 6 4 -4 5 -6 6 -5 5 -3 -3

4

The minute you let her under your skin, then you begin to make it

better.

4 7 -7 -6 6 6 -5 -6 7 -6 7 -5

And any time you feel the pain, hey, Jude, refrain

7 -6 6 -5 6 -6 6 -5 5 -4 4

Don't carry the world upon your shoulders.

4 7 -6 -6 6 6 -5 -6 7 -6 7 -5

For now you know that it's a fool who plays it cool

7 -6 6 -5 6 -6 6 -5 5 -4 4 4 6 -6 -7 -6 -7 -7 7 -8

-8

By making his world a little co ld er. da da da da da da da da da

Harmonica Tabs for Traditional Songs

These tabs are songs you're sure to know. From traditional Irish folk songs to holiday music, these tunes are simple, universal, and a great way to get yourself familiar with your harmonica before braving more complex music (*Today's 20 most popular songs,* n.d.):

Black Velvet Band (Chorus) - Traditional Irish

Key: C

6 6 6 5 -5 6 -5 5

Oh, her eyes they shone like diamonds,

-4 4 -4 5 4 -3 3 3

Youd think she was queen of the land,

6 -5 5 5 3 3 -3 4 -4 5

And her hair hung over her shoulders,

4 -4 5 -5 -3 4 -4 4

Tied up with a black velvet band.

Botany Bay - Traditional Irish

Key: A

Verse 1

4 -4 5 6 6 -4 -5 -5 5 4

Fare-are-well to Old Eng-land for-ev-er

6 5 6 7 -5 -6 7 6

Fare-well to my old pals as well

-6 -7 7 -7 7 -8 7 -6 6 5 4

Fare-are-well to the well known Old Ba-il-ey

4 -4 5 6 6 -4 -5 5 4

Where I once used to look such a swell!

Chorus

6 -5 5 6 6 -4 -5 -5 5 -4 4

Sing-ing too ra la oo ra lie ad-dit-y

6 -5 5 6 7 -5 -6 7 6

Sing-ing too ra la oo ra lie ay

-6 -7 7 -7 7 -8 7 -6 6 5 4

Sing-ing too ra la oo ra lie ad-dit-y

4 -4 5 6 6 -4 -5 5 4

We're bou-nd for Bot-an-y Bay!

Danny Boy - Traditional Irish

Key: C

-7 7 -8 8 -8 8

6 -6 -7 7 -7 -7

Oh, Danny- boy, the pipes,

-10 9 8 -8 7 -6 7 8 -9 9 -10 9 8 7 8

-8

-6 6 -6 6 5 4 6 -6 -7 7 -6 6 5 4 5

-4

the pipes are calling from glen to glen, and down the mountain side.

-7 8 -8 8 -8 8 -10 9 8 -8 7 -6

-3 4 -4 5 -4 5 -6 6 5 -4 4 4

The summer's gone and all the roses falling.

-7 7 -8 8 -9 8 -8 7 -8 7

-3 4 -4 5 -6 6 5 4 -4 4

It's you, it's you must go and I must bide.

6 -6 -7 7 -7 -7 -6 6 -6 6 5 4

But come ye back when summer's in the meadow

6 -6 -7 7 -7 -7 -6 6 5 -4

or when the valley's hushed and white with snow.

6 6 6 8 -8 -8 7 -6 7 6 5 4

It's I'll be here in sunshine or in shadow.

-3 4 -4 5 -6 6 5 -4 7 -6 -7 7

Oh, Danny- boy. Oh, Danny- boy, I love you so.

God Rest Ye Merry, Gentlemen - Traditional Christmas

Key: C

5 5 -7 -7 -6 6 -5 5

God rest ye merry, gen-tle-men

-4 5 -5 6 -6 -7

Let nothing you dismay

5 5 -7 -7 -6 6 -5 5

Re-mem-ber, Christ, our Sa-v-ior

-4 5 -5 6 -6 -7

Was born on Christmas day

-7 7 -6 -7 7 -8 8 -7 -7

To save us all from Satan's power

-6 6 5 -5 6 -6

When we were gone astray

6 -6 -7 7 -7 -7 6 -5 5

O--- tidings of comfort and joy,

6 -6 -7 -8 8 -7 6 -5 5

O---- tidings of comfort and joy

God, Save the Queen - British National Anthem

Key: C

4 4 <<-4 <<-3 4 <<-4

God save our grac-ious Queen

5 5 <<-5 5 <<-4 4

Long live our no-ble Queen,

<-4 4 <<-3 4

God save the queen,

6 6 6 6 <-55 <<-5 <-5<<-5 5 <<-4 4

Send her vic-tor-ious hap-py and glo-ri-ous

4 <<-4 <<-4 5 <<-4 4 <<-3

Long to-oo rei--gn over us

<<-4 <<-4 4 <<-3 4

Go--od save the Queen.

Good Christian Men, Rejoice - Traditional Christmas

Key: G

7 7 7 8 -9 9 -10 9

Good Christian men, re-jo-i-ce

9 7 7 8 -9 9 -10 9

with heart and soul and vo-i-ce.

9 -10 9 -9 8 -8 7

Give ye heed to what we say:

7 7 -8 -8 8 -8 7 -8 8

News! news! Jesus Christ is born today!

9 -10 9 -9 8 -8 7

Ox and ass before Him bow,

7 -8 -8 8 -8 7 -8 8

and He is in the manger now.

-6 -6 -7 -7 7

Christ is born today!

8 8 -8 -8 7

Christ is born today!

Happy Birthday - Traditional

Key: C

6 6 -6 6 7 -7

Hap-py birth-day to you,

6 6 -6 6 -8 7

Hap-py birth-day to you,

6 6 9 8 7 -7 -6

Hap-py birth-day to ___ ___

-9 -9 8 7 -8 7

Hap-py birth-day to you.

Hush Little Baby - Traditional Lullaby

Key: C

3 5 5 5 -5 5 -4 -4 -4

Hush, little baby, don't say a word,

3 3 -4 -4 -4 -4 5 -4 4 4

Mama's gonna buy you a mockingbird.

3 5 5 -5 5 -4 -4

If that mockingbird don't sing

3 3 -4 -4 -4 -4 5 -4 4 4

Mama's gonna buy you a diamond ring....

Old Soldiers Never Die (Chorus) - 1940s Patriotic

Key: C

7 -7 -6 6 7 6

Old Sol-diers nev-er die,

7 -6 -5 -6 6 5

Nev-er die, nev-er die,

7 -7 -6 6 7 6

Old Sol-diers nev-er die,

7 7 -6 -5 6 5

They sim-ply fade a-way,

7 7 -6 -5 6 5

They sim-ply fade a-way.

The Bear Went Over the Mountain - Traditional Children's

Key: C

4 5 5 5 -4 5 -5 5

The Bear went ov-er the moun-tain

5 -4 -4 -4 4 -4 5 4

The Bear went ov-er the moun-tain

4 5 5 5 -4 5 -5 -6

The Bear went ov-er the moun-tain

-6 6 -5 5 -4 4

To see what he could see

4 6 6 -6 -6 6

To see what he could see

-5 5 5 -5 -5 5

To see what he could see

-5 5 5 5 -5 -5 5 -6

The ot-her side of the moun-tain,

4 5 5 5 -4 5 -5 -6

The ot-her side of the moun-tain

-6 6 -5 5 -4 4

Was all that he could see

The Overlander - Traditional Irish

Key: C

5 -5 6 -6 6 5 7

There's a trade you all know well,

5 6 6 -6 6 5 5 -4

It's bring-ing the cat-tle o-ver.

5 6 6 5 4 4 7 7 -6

On ev'ry track, to the Gulf and back,

-6 6 6 -4 -5 5 4

Men know the Queens-land dro-ver.

7 7 7 -7 -7 -7 7

So pass, the bil-ly round, boys,

6 6 6 -6 6 6 -4

Don't let the pint pot stand there.

5 -5 6 -6 6 5 7

For to-night, we'll drink the health,

-6 6 6 6 -5 5 4

Of ev'ry O-ver-land-er.

Old Macdonald Had a Farm - Traditional Children's

Key: C

7 7 7 6 -6 -6 6

8 8 -8 -8 7 6 7 7 7 6 -6 -6 6

8 8 -8 -8 7

Chapter 6:
Building a Collection

2211438. (n.d.). *harmonica instruments* [Photograph]. Pixabay.
https://pixabay.com/photos/harmonica-instruments-music-1369449/

As you start to improve, experiment, and expand your abilities, you'll probably find yourself in the market for a second harmonica. Most people make their second harmonica an A diatonic, but harmonicas in the keys of D, F, and G are also quite popular. Armed with a C, A, and G harmonica, there will be very little music you can't easily play in 1st or 2nd position.

Your next harmonica purchase will largely depend on your ambitions as a future player. If you want to play blues or rock music, then it makes sense to continue with diatonic harmonicas. Traditional or folk musicians will also likely want to stay with diatonic harmonicas. Though diatonic harmonicas are sometimes viewed as "basic," there's a great deal of room to expand as a player using this harmonica alone. Depending on the harmonica you began with, you may want to purchase a better quality C harmonica from a serious brand now that you have mastered the basics. You may want to purchase a harmonica tuned to a different musical key to start experimenting with music in new keys and positions. You may want to purchase a harmonica with an alternative tuning, such as a country tuning or natural minor. Or you may want to expand beyond the diatonic, and jump into the world of chromatic or even tremolo harmonicas.

Harmonicas tuned to other major musical keys are by far the easiest to find. A simple online search of "major diatonic harmonicas" will link you to hundreds of harmonicas tuned to all 12 musical keys. Almost every diatonic harmonica you'll find in a local music store will be tuned to a major key. However, if you enjoy playing music in minor keys, you may want to look for harmonicas with special minor tunings. In particular, folk musicians may want to consider this option, as many folk songs are written in minor keys (Hertzberg, 2020).

So if you decide you want to stick with a major diatonic harmonica for now, how do you decide which key to choose? Most likely, the harmonica you're using right now is a C harmonica. Depending on how you acquired this instrument, you may want to upgrade to something that's higher-quality or better suited to your playing style. You may want to purchase something with a more interesting aesthetic or made of different materials. The beauty of the harmonica is that it's not a very expensive instrument. Even a high quality or uniquely built harmonica won't cost that much compared to other kinds of custom instruments. It's very common for people to start learning the harmonica on instruments that were gifted or passed on to them. So it's perfectly natural to make your second harmonica a C harmonica that's more tailored to your personal needs.

Generally speaking, the lower the key, the more difficult it is to play. The same is true, however, for keys that are extremely high. Moving forward, then, you'll probably want to choose a key that's still somewhere in the middle range, close to C. G is the lowest key, and F is the highest, so these are probably not the best choices for a second harmonica. Jumping straight into a specialty key or alternative tuning is probably not the best option, either. If you want to try a different key, I would recommend moving one whole step up or down from the key of C. If you want to move slightly up in pitch, that would mean getting a D harmonica. If you want to move slightly down in pitch, that would mean getting a B harmonica. With a D harmonica, 2nd position puts you in the key of A, a very common key for blues and rock music.

The most common second choice for serious harmonica players, however, is an A harmonica. On this tuning, 2nd position puts you in the key of E, a very melodic, but slightly challenging, key. From an A harmonica, it's much easier to progress to a G harmonica, which is an extremely common key for blues music.

But the key is not the only decision you have to make when purchasing a new harmonica. Now that you're more familiar with how a harmonica works and sounds, you can be a bit more discerning when it comes to choosing a brand. Some brands are universally reputable, while others are better for certain needs or styles. You will often find that seasoned players tend to have certain brands that they favor over others. A good rule of thumb is that, with harmonicas, you typically get what you pay for. More often than not, the cheaper the harmonica, the lower the quality.

A Note on Hohner Harmonicas

Though there are many reputable harmonica manufacturers world-wide, it's difficult to talk about harmonica manufacturers without talking about Hohner. For blues players, especially, this brand is widely considered the best in the business (Hertzberg, 2020).

Hohner Special 20

If you want to stick with a C harmonica and upgrade the quality of your instrument, you may want to consider adding a Hohner Special 20 to your harmonica collection. This is commonly advertised as a beginner harmonica, but it's of such high quality that it will last you well into a professional career. The plastic comb makes it both extremely easy to clean and long-lasting. If you are currently working with a wooden comb, making the switch to a plastic comb is advisable, as wooden combs generally have much shorter lifespans. This is an excellent choice for those who are looking for an affordable and durable diatonic harmonica.

Hohner Marine Band Deluxe

For many, this is considered the "classic" Hohner harmonica. If you'd like to stick with a more traditional sound and style, you may want to consider making the Marine Band Deluxe your second harmonica. Despite its name, the tuning of this harmonica works extremely well for blues music.

Hohner Marine Band Crossover

This is an updated version of the more traditional Marine Band Deluxe model. This harmonica has a bamboo comb, giving it the look of a wooden comb without the typical problems. This model comes in various keys, but the tuning is a bit unusual, so it may not be the best choice for those who are committed to playing 2nd Position blues.

Hohner Marine Band Classic

This is the original Marine Band model and is still the go-to instrument for many professional blues players. This harmonica model has been copied many times and not without cause. It's simple, classic style makes it extremely easy to play. It's pearwood comb is partially sealed, lending it an extra level of durability. However, a wood comb is still a wood comb. After years of use, you will probably start to experience some swelling with this model. The reed plates in this model are nailed to the comb, so if you're looking to customize or change the tuning on your harmonica, this model may not be the best option.

Starting Your Collection

If you plan to play by and for yourself, then your choice of harmonica is purely up to personal preference. But if you are looking to play professionally or jam with other people, then the more keys you have available, the more easily you'll fit into any musical situation.

If you're looking to play in a more serious way, then there are a few questions to ask yourself when choosing the key of your next harmonica. The first question to ask yourself, of course, is, "Will I be playing alone, or would I like to play with other people in the future?"

If you are learning the harmonica simply for your own personal enjoyment, you can make your next purchase in whatever key you wish to learn next. When playing solo, there are restrictions on what you can learn or experiment with. However, if you're looking to play with other people, then you'll want to familiarize yourself with the keys in which that group or band typically performs, and choose a harmonica accordingly.

You should also ask yourself what genre or style of music you'd like to play. As you now know, different styles of music lend themselves better to certain keys and positions. Traditional and folk music tends to be played in the 1st position. If this is the kind of music you want to learn, then you'll want to purchase a harmonica that's tuned to the key in which most of the songs you want to play are composed. You already have a C harmonica, which means you can play 1st position in the key of C, so what other keys have you been encountering as you start to branch out?

Blues and rock music, on the other hand, tend to be played in the 2nd position. If this is the kind of music you want to play, you'll want to choose a harmonica not based on its tuning key but its key in 2nd position. If you are a blues player, you may very well wish to purchase a better quality C harmonica, as G in the 2nd position is a very common style of play for blues musicians.

Without a doubt, if you wish to play blues or rock music seriously, then you will need to consider the 2nd position tuning of any future harmonicas you wish to purchase. Even if you don't prefer playing 2nd Position right now, it's something you will encounter over and over again in these genres.

If you're shy about purchasing a harmonica in a new key, remember that the pattern of the notes and chords will be the same on any major diatonic harmonica. So if you've learned to play "Jingle Bells" on your C harmonica, you can still play "Jingle Bells" on any major diatonic harmonica using the same blow and draw patterns. This is not true, however, if you decide to branch out to an alternative tuning. Minor tunings will change the pattern of the notes on the harmonica. If you're thinking about purchasing a harmonica with an alternative tuning, consider that you will have to relearn the blow and draw patterns of every song you've already learned (*Which Keys of Harmonica Should I Buy to Get Started?*, n.d.).

The three most common tunings for diatonic harmonicas are C, A, and G. If you have harmonicas in just those three keys, you will be able to sit down and play almost any song with almost any group of people. If you add a D harmonica to that collection, there will be very few musical situations in which you find yourself struggling to play in the right key. Remember that each new harmonica you buy will come with new keys in the 2nd, 3rd, and 4th positions. So, a purchase of just one new harmonica can provide you with a whole new world of musical options.

Most serious players end up with a small collection of diatonic harmonicas in a range of keys. Because they are much more modestly priced than other instruments, building a harmonica collection is a relatively easy thing to do. For your first few harmonicas, I would recommend trying instruments from several different brands to get a feel for which ones you like the best.

Hohner, Fender, and Swan are commonly considered the "best" for harmonica manufacturers. Lee Oskar is another reputable brand with an astonishing variety of diatonic harmonicas in every key, plus several alternative tunings for specialized genres like gypsy jazz and Eastern folk music. The Blues Session model by Seydel has a unique sound because its reeds are made of steel, rather than the typical brass, so it may be a good choice if you want to upgrade your C harmonica.

However, if you are a committed jazz musician, you may want to consider purchasing a chromatic harmonica. Unlike diatonic harmonicas, chromatic harmonicas come pre-installed with reed plates capable of playing all of the notes on a chromatic scale. It has a button-activated gear-shift that enables the player to move extremely easily between keys, essentially condensing the musical ability of 12 differently tuned diatonic harmonicas into one single instrument.

Chromatic harmonicas are much more difficult to play than diatonic harmonicas, and they have a slightly different sound because their reeds are much bigger. The size of the reeds makes it difficult to bend and overbend on chromatic harmonicas. While these techniques are less necessary because of the instrument's built-in musical range, they are still important, especially if you wish to continue playing blues. Despite these difficulties,, many renowned blues players, including Little Walter and Rod Piazza, used chromatic harmonicas to beautiful effect. However, if you are a blues player, a chromatic harmonica would not be a wise choice for a second harmonica.

If you're a jazz or classical musician, you will ultimately find that it's much easier to play technically complex music on a chromatic harmonica. Once you master the technique of bending on a chromatic harmonica, there's very little music that you can't play by sight. The additional difficulty of playing the chromatic harmonica will mean a great deal of extra practice, but if you're committed to jazz or classical music, then hours of practice is an inevitable part of your playing experience. And if you've already mastered the basics on a diatonic harmonica, graduating to a chromatic will be much easier. This is especially true if you're comfortable playing in all 12 positions on your diatonic harmonica. Like diatonic harmonicas, chromatic harmonicas come tuned to a specific key (typically C or G). However, chromatic harmonicas have the inherent ability to play all of the notes in a chromatic scale, with much less need for bending or overbending to reach certain notes. The Hohner 280/64 Chromonica 64 Chromatic Harmonica is an excellent choice for both blues and jazz musicians seeking bigger tones and more musical versatility (*How to Choose a Harmonica*, 2018).

Recommended Harmonicas for Different Requirements

If your first harmonica was a gift or inheritance, you didn't have to go through purchasing one your first time around. But once you start shopping, it's very easy to get overwhelmed by the sheer range of harmonicas that are out there on the market. Inevitably, this means doing a bit of research and a little self-reflection. Every time you purchase a new instrument, whether it's your first or your 10th, you want to make sure it's the right instrument for you and your needs. If you're looking to become a great blues musician, you probably shouldn't be shopping for chromatic harmonicas. On the other hand, if you want to play jazz or rock music, on the other hand, then a blues harmonica may not be the right call.

Learning which harmonicas are best for certain needs and requirements will help you to make a purchase that's right for you. In many ways, buying your second harmonica is even more difficult than acquiring your first. At this point, you know a lot more about how the harmonica works and in which direction you want to expand your abilities. With that being said, you also understand just how many options there are for the type of music you wish to play.

The two main things to consider when purchasing a harmonica are what kind of music are you playing and for what purpose? Different genres and styles lend themselves better to different keys, types of harmonicas, and brands. If you're eager to improve your musical range and technical proficiency, you may want to consider moving right up to a chromatic harmonica. If you're looking to play blues or jazz, on the other hand, you may want to start purchasing diatonic harmonicas in different keys (*Best harmonica beginner's guide with top 10 harmonica reviews 2020,* 2020).

If you're a casual or solo player, then you'll want to stick with diatonic harmonicas for now. If you are a serious player or want to start playing professionally, you may want to consider experimenting with different types of harmonicas. However, if you're typically playing melodies or melodic accompaniments, then diatonic harmonicas are still going to be your best option.

For a blues player looking for a quality diatonic harmonica:

I would recommend the Hohner Marine Band Harmonica in the key of C. Though it has a wooden comb, this is an extremely well-built harmonica with a classic blues sound. For blues players throughout the years, this has been considered the go-to harmonica for serious musicians. This harmonica is so beloved by blues players because its design makes it very easy to bend.

Pros:

- A versatile harmonica that can play in a range of styles;
- Easy bending and natural bluesy tone, and;
- Very affordable.

Cons:

- Since this is a diatonic harmonica, you may want to purchase this harmonica in a different key.

For someone looking to see if they enjoy playing the harmonica:

I would recommend the Hohner Blues Band 1501BX Harmonica in the keys of C, G, or A. This extremely affordable harmonica is a great first or second instrument. This harmonica is one of the most popular Hohner models this year. It's a quality instrument to experiment with to determine if the harmonica is something you want to stick with for the long-term (*Best harmonicas guide with top 10 harmonica reviews 2020*, 2020).

Pros:

- Very affordable, and;
- Easy to play.

Cons:

- It is not a very stylish harmonica.

For someone already proficient in playing a diatonic harmonica:

I would recommend the Hohner 270BX Super Chromonica in the key of C. This simple chromatic harmonica is a good step up for musicians who wish to expand beyond diatonic harmonicas. This extremely popular model has a wooden body and a quality sound.

Pros:

- A full chromatic range of play;
- Stylish wooden body, and;
- Easy to learn and play.

Cons:

- Expensive, and;
- Similarly priced harmonicas from different brands are typically much higher quality.

For someone looking to play the harmonica on a budget:

I would recommend the Fender Blues Deluxe in any key. This harmonica is specifically designed by Fender to sound great when accompanying blues guitar. It's an extremely comfortable and easy instrument to play. However, its quality ensures that it makes a long-lasting addition to any harmonica collection (*Best harmonica beginner's guide with top 10 harmonica reviews 2020*, 2020).

Pros:

- Very affordable;
- Comfortable to play, and;
- A distinctive bluesy sound.

Cons:

- It is not as popular or recognizable as other, bigger harmonica brands.

For a player who wishes to both look and sound stylish:

I would recommend the Fender Blues DeVille in the key of C. With a PVC comb and bronze reeds, this Fender harmonica has a slightly different tone than other diatonic harmonicas. And its black and gold color scheme looks extremely sleek and stylish on stage.

Pros:

- Well-made;
- Unique blues sound, and;
- Excellent quality of sound.

Cons:

- The bronze reeds make high notes slightly more difficult to play than on normal harmonicas.

For someone looking to play the chromatic harmonica on a budget:

I would recommend the Swan Chromatic Harmonica SW1040 in the key of C. This quality chromatic harmonica is extremely affordable. Its price comes from the materials, not the quality, as it's built entirely of metal. A relatively basic model, this is a great first chromatic harmonica for those who want to expand beyond diatonic harmonicas. And its low price also makes it a good option for those who want to experiment with a chromatic harmonica to see if they like it.

Pros:

- Great for pop and folk players;
- Extremely affordable for a chromatic harmonica, and;
- The full-metal body gives it a stylish appearance.

Cons:

- It is not difficult to play, but not beginner-friendly, either.

For someone on a budget looking to play the blues:

I would recommend the Swan Blues diatonic harmonica in the key of C or G. This extremely affordable harmonica is designed with a blues sound in mind. If you're looking to upgrade the harmonica you've been learning on, a harmonica in the key of C will help you continue learning while practicing your blues style. If you'd like to branch out to other keys, I would recommend getting this harmonica in the key of G, which will give you the option to play many blues songs in 1st or 2nd Position (*Best harmonica beginner's guide with top 10 harmonica reviews 2020*, 2020).

Pros:

- Very affordable;
- Distinctive bluesy sound;
- Easy to play, and;
- The plastic comb makes it a long-lasting instrument.

Cons:

- A very basic model with limited player features, so it is not suitable if you want to branch out beyond blues music.

For someone who wishes to play in multiple musical keys with relative ease:

I would recommend the Swan diatonic harmonica set of seven. This is a boxed set of seven different harmonicas, each tuned to a different key. This allows you to obtain seven harmonicas in one purchase and gives you the ability to learn on seven different keys. Considering you're purchasing seven instruments all at once, this is also quite an affordable purchase.

Pros:

- Very affordable;
- An easy way to expand your range of play;
- Gives you all the tools you need to become a proficient diatonic harmonica player, and;
- Great for both jazz and blues players.

Cons:

- These harmonicas are relatively basic in design, and so they aren't suitable for more advanced effects like echoes or bass notes.

Chapter 7:
Cleaning and Maintaining Your Harmonica

The more you play, the more important it becomes to care for your instrument properly. Taking good care of your harmonica is critical at all times. And even with the best care and attention, you may still need to do some maintenance work on your instrument in the future. Thankfully, harmonicas are not terribly complex instruments, and most of the technical problems they experience are relatively easy to fix. Basic care and daily maintenance of the harmonica is even easier. Most minor problems are so simple you can fix them yourself without paying or consulting a professional (*Fix Your Harmonica*, n.d.).

The lifespan of your harmonica is dependent on a number of different factors, including how often you play, how hard you play, what kind of music you play, the model of the harmonica, and how much moisture it's exposed to. If you're the type of player that exclusively favors one harmonica at a time, then it's not uncommon to expect that you'll have to replace your harmonica every year. This is another reason many serious players have a collection of harmonicas, rather than relying on one at a time. If you have a variety of harmonicas, all of which you properly care for, it's not uncommon for one harmonica to last up to 30 years in perfect playing condition. The secret is in how you care for it every day.

Maintaining the performance of your harmonica is simple but extremely important. The three most common reasons that harmonicas have to be replaced are rust, particulates (lint, particles of food, etc.), and blowing too hard when you play it. Moisture is deadly to harmonicas, and rust can make your harmonica impossible to play in as little as six months if you aren't careful. Think about your harmonica as if it were a car. It, too, has moving mechanical parts, and the more you use it, the more wear-and-tear it has to endure. Like a car, the individual parts of the harmonica will deteriorate with usage, rust, poor fuel (being played with a dirty mouth), and stress (Allen, n.d.).

No matter what, the more you play a harmonica, the shorter its life will be. But many beginning players damage their harmonicas by blowing too hard, especially when trying to bend. Even correct bending puts stress on the reeds, and so blues players tend to burn through harmonicas faster than musicians playing other styles. Though most harmonicas use brass reeds, stainless steel is by far the most durable material. But the number one killer of harmonicas is moisture.

All of this means that, if you want your harmonica to last 30 years or more, you need to play it softly, play it very rarely, dry it immediately after you play it, and store it in a cool, dry, airtight place. While this is certainly possible, it's not very practical for most serious players, even if you have a big collection of harmonicas.

A harmonica to last 30 years or more in perfect playing condition. But the reality is that you're probably going to be replacing your harmonicas much more frequently than that. If you're a blues player who tends to favor one particular harmonica, you can expect to get a new harmonica every year. The unfortunate truth is that the harmonicas that tend to last for several years are the ones you play the least. And, since bending puts stress on the reeds, if you play a genre that doesn't require a lot of bending, you're also likely to get a few more years out of your harmonicas than a blues or jazz player.

In theory, you could replace the reeds in your harmonica when they become worn, but this costs more money than buying a brand new harmonica. If you learn how to replace the reeds or the reed plates yourself, you can potentially get many more years out of the same harmonica. Some harmonicas even come with replaceable reed plates to make this process even easier. If you're interested in replacing your reeds, you'll want to pay attention to draw 4, 5, and 7. These are the reeds that tend to wear out the fastest, as these are the notes that are typically played the most.

Besides learning how to replace your own reeds, there are a few simpler strategies you can employ to increase the lifespan of your favorite harmonica greatly (*Care and Maintenance of a Harmonica,* n.d.):

Brush Your Teeth Before Playing

Before playing the harmonica, your mouth should always be clean. Food particles, coffee, and other residue or moisture from your mouth can cause a great deal of damage if they enter the body of the harmonica.

Resist the Urge to Drink Before Playing

It's not the alcohol itself that will damage your harmonica—it's your inability to regulate your breathing. Blowing too hard is a sure way to damage your harmonica before its time, and even the most seasoned players tend to huff and puff after a few beers.

Don't Share Your Instruments

Don't let anyone else have a go on your favorite or high-performance instruments, even if you're sure they'll treat them delicately.

Let Your Harmonica Air-Dry After Playing

Allowing your harmonica to lay out in the open and air-dry for 10–15 minutes after playing can go a long way toward reducing rust.

Slap Out Residual Moisture

Another way to reduce moisture build-up is to gently tap the body of the harmonica against the palm of your hand after playing to release any residual moisture trapped inside.

Store Your Harmonicas in Cases

Coins, lint, and even humidity can damage your harmonica, so it's important to store them in cases when they aren't in use. If you want to carry your harmonica in your pocket and you don't have a case, even a simple ziplock bag will protect it from harm.

Don't Blow Too Hard

It can't be stated enough—you don't need to blow that hard to get a big sound out of your harmonica. Where many beginner players tend to damage their reeds is when they first attempt bending. Learning to open and close the muscles in your throat will help you magnify the sound without having to blow any harder. Even the grittiest blues players don't need to blow that hard to have complete control over their bends. This is the number one way that people damage their harmonicas, and it's something that is extremely avoidable. This is why beginners should start out on a good quality harmonica, but not exorbitantly expensive. You don't want to drop a lot of money on a harmonica, only to replace it in six months because the reeds are worn out.

Don't Play Your Harmonica While It's Cold

If you need, place it under your armpit for a few minutes to warm it up before you play.

Do Not Leave Your Harmonica to Dry In a Hot Place

Dryers and stoves can damage your harmonica. Letting it sit out in the open air is the best way to safely dry your harmonica after you've cleaned it (Yerxa, 2016b).

Use a Gentle Material to Wipe Your Mouthpiece

Gauze, microfiber cloths for glasses, and even toothbrushes are great materials to use to wipe down your mouthpiece after playing.

Handle Your Instrument with Care

It does without saying that dropping your harmonica is a great way to damage it, especially if you drop it on a hard surface like cement or a wooden stage.

Often, players will notice that just one or two notes will suddenly stop working. This is most likely due to a build-up of saliva in the comb. When you play, you should always make sure that your head remains upright to prevent saliva from leaking down into the body of the harmonica. If you find you have trouble holding your head up while trying to read music or tabs, it might be a good idea to invest in a music stand.

Though it sounds gross, many professional players learn to let saliva pool inside the mouth under their tongue and frequently swallow to prevent that saliva from leaking into the harmonica. If you find that a few of your reeds are clogged with saliva, try slapping out the moisture by gently tapping the body of the harmonica against the palm of your hand. If that doesn't work, try rapidly alternating between the blow and the draw note to loosen the moisture. When all else fails, put the harmonica in a place where it can dry very quickly, especially next to a fan or air conditioner (Allen, n.d.).

Tuning and Cleaning Your Harmonica

Over time, even the most well cared for harmonicas will start to fall out of tune. At this point, many people start shopping for a new instrument, but if you want to get a longer life out of your harmonica, you can learn to tune your harmonica yourself. Tuning a harmonica is not particularly difficult, but it requires some basic tools and intimate working knowledge of your harmonica's individual parts. Remember to only tune reeds after doing other maintenance work, such as embossing the slots or aligning them. These and other maintenance activities can change the tuning.

The basics of tuning are simple—you're either looking to raise or lower the pitch of an individual reed. To lower the pitch of a given note, you can remove a small amount of metal from the surface of the reed at the base. Alternatively, you can add a small amount of solder or heavy putty to the surface of the reed at the tip. To raise the pitch, remove a small amount of metal from the tip. Remember that the tip is the part of the harmonica that sticks out into the slot.

No matter what, if you want to tune your harmonica, you'll need direct access to the reeds whose tones you wish to change. It's nearly impossible to tune your harmonica without being able to see and touch the reeds you're working with. In diatonic harmonicas, the reeds are mounted on one side of the reed plate. This will be the side that you would need to access.

When you first remove your harmonica covers, the draw reeds will be the ones facing toward you. The blow reeds are located inside the comb, so if these are the reeds you want to change, you'll need to detach the reed plates from the comb. It is possible to tune blow reeds while they're still attached to the comb, but it's extremely difficult. By detaching the reed plates, you'll be far less likely to damage the reeds (Yerxa, 2016d).

Tuning Your Harmonica, Step-by-Step:

First, place a shim between the reed and the reed plate. A thin piece of metal or plastic will work fine. Even a stiff piece of paper can provide the support you need. Just remember that the purpose of the shim is to support the reed and that using a shim that's too thick can cause you to accidentally pry the base of the reed off of the reed plate altogether.

To tune your reed, you'll need to remove metal from a certain part of the reed. To do this, gently stroke it with a sanding detailer with a medium-to-fine grit sanding belt. If you aren't sure, err on the side of a finer grit.

Be careful to sand in a very small area along the surface of the reed. Where you choose to sand will depend on whether you intend to raise or lower the pitch. Be sure to sand lengthwise—sanding across the reed can cause burrs that create friction with the edge of the slot and weaken the reed overall.

Don't press too hard when sanding, as this can change the shape of the reed. If you're sanding the tip of the reed, it's best to sand outward. If you sand inward, you run the risk of bending the reed. Always be extremely delicate while you're sanding. If you're sanding near the base of the reed, you can feel safe to sand inward.

Every so often, pause to test the tuning. Do this by removing the shim, plucking the reed, and assembling the harmonica to test it. Remember that warm reeds tend to vibrate at a much lower pitch than cold reeds. When you play, your breath warms up the reeds, so it's advisable to tune reeds that are warm. Storing the reed plates on an electric heating pad for 10–15 minutes before you start tuning will help warm them up, and working in a warm environment will help keep the reeds warmed up while you work (Yerxa, 2016d).

Cleaning Your Harmonica Without Taking It Apart

Unlike other instruments, harmonicas must be regularly cleaned to keep them working at an optimal level. However, incorrectly cleaning your harmonica can ultimately cause more damage than it prevents.

Thankfully, you don't have to completely take apart your harmonica to keep it in clean and working order. A regular washing routine will keep your harmonica clean of saliva. Depending on how often you play, you should wash your harmonica at least once a month, if not every week. Though it seems counterintuitive to wash an instrument that's so vulnerable to rust, if done properly, this procedure will greatly extend the life of your instrument. Remember that washing is only appropriate for harmonicas with combs made of plastic or metal alloys. Combs made of steel or wood will be damaged by even a quick rinse (*How to Clean a Harmonica*, n.d.).

To wash your harmonica, give it a quick rinse in lukewarm water. Make sure that the water is not too hot or ice cold. Then tap the body gently against the palm of your hand with the mouthpiece facing down to clear out any water that may have gotten trapped inside. Once this has been done, leave your harmonica out to dry. Make sure it's completely dry before packing it away in its case.

If your harmonica has a wooden or steel comb, then washing is not an option. Instead, gently clean your harmonica with a soft dry brush. A toothbrush works great for this purpose, as the bristles are typically soft, and the brush is slender enough to get inside the mouth holes.

Giving Your Harmonica a Full Clean

Once every three to six months, you should perform a full clean on your harmonica.

First, remove the screws fastening down the cover plates with an appropriately sized screwdriver to take apart the harmonica safely. Keep these in a small bowl or another safe place, as you'll need them to put the harmonica back together again. Once the cover plates have been detached, wiped them down with alcohol spray and a clean cloth.

Next, remove the reed plates and leave them to soak for about 30 minutes in lukewarm water with just a few drops of vinegar or citric acid. While the reed plates are soaking, wash the comb with soap and lukewarm water. Gently remove any deposits by scrubbing them off with a soft brush. If your harmonica has a wooden comb, don't wash it—simply scrubbing it with the dry brush will be enough to clean it.

When the reed plates have finished soaking, brush them clean with a soft brush. Ensure that your brush strokes are always up and down the reeds, not across them sideways. Once you've finished brushing, give the reed plates one more quick rinse, and then lay them out in a safe place to dry.

Make sure all the pieces of the harmonica are completely dry before you put them all back together. When tightening the screws, make sure that they are secure enough to keep the harmonica airtight, but be wary of screwing them too tight. This can cause the comb to crack and damage the harmonica permanently.

Tips, Tricks, and Common Mistakes to Avoid when Cleaning Your Harmonica

Due to health regulations, your local music shop cannot exchange or refund a harmonica that has already been opened. Once you've purchased your harmonica, it's considered used, and that means you'll have to return it directly to the manufacturer for warranty services.

This is a fairly common policy for all wind instruments, for the obvious reason that you play them by putting your mouth on them. But more often than not, if you feel that your harmonica is "defective" or not working as well as it should, that's a good indicator that you're just not cleaning it as often as you should be. Regularly washing and brushing your harmonica will greatly extend its life and improve the quality of its performance.

Because your harmonica is mouth-blown, simply playing the instrument slowly wears down its tonal quality and pushes it out of tune. Even the cleanest mouth isn't clean—at least, not by harmonica standards. Every person's body chemistry is different, and human saliva carries our chemical footprint, including small traces of sugar and other contaminants. These chemical contaminants combine with residue from the food we eat and congeal on the surface of the harmonica's internal parts. It may sound gross, but there's no way around it. Buildup on the reeds, over time, will cause the reed to fall out of tune. Heavy residue on the reed plates can also compromise the harmonica's sound quality. And it's not just saliva and food. Particles of hair and pocket lint are common culprits when it comes to a lackluster harmonica sound. So before you decide that your harmonica needs to be retuned, try washing it first and see if that restores the quality of the sound.

If you want to prevent all of this, there's a simple solution—regularly washing and brushing your harmonica. If it's a harmonica that you only play once or twice a year, you should consider giving it a quick washing before you play. Even harmonicas that have been sitting "safely" in their cases are vulnerable to rust, humidity, and dust. Weekly washing and brushing will also keep your harmonica looking shiny and new, an important quality if you're playing in front of an audience. Improperly cleaning your harmonica can cause more damage than it prevents. Always be very gentle with the various pieces of your harmonica. The last thing you want is to compromise your harmonica in an attempt to extend its life. It should also be noted that cleaning the harmonica also eats away at its lifespan. It just eats away at it *less* than rust or food build-up does.

If your harmonica is nailed together (not screwed), use a pocket knife or another instrument with a thin blade. Gently push the nail between the cover and the reed plate, making sure to stay as far as you can from the reeds themselves. Use the blade to pry the cover plate away from the reed plate gently, and then use a small pair of pliers to pull the nail free. Even if you're using a screwdriver, be wary of the reeds whenever you remove the cover plate (How to Clean and Seal a Harmonica, 2020b).

Many players like to clean their harmonicas from the top-down, one piece at a time, to offer the reeds the maximum amount of protection. This would mean first removing and cleaning the top cover plate, then the top reed plate, then the comb, then the bottom reed plate, and ending with the bottom cover plate. This can sometimes take a bit longer, but it's much safer. This method is especially recommended if this is your first time giving your harmonica a full clean.

When removing the reed plates, take extreme care to avoid damaging either the reeds or the comb. If the reed plates are nailed to the comb, you can use a blade to remove them the same way you used it to remove the cover plates. However, remember that the reed plates and comb are much more delicate than the cover plates. If possible, try to slide the blade of your knife between the nail and the reed plate to loosen it, and then use pliers to pull it free. Only try to insert the blade between the reed plate and the comb if you absolutely have to. The sharpness of the blade can scratch or otherwise damage the comb. This process requires even more care when removing the draw reeds, as the reeds will be facing upwards and therefore be even more vulnerable. Whether your reed plates are screwed or nailed, be very careful when handling tools around your reeds. One slip of the screwdriver can accidentally damage a reed, rendering your harmonica virtually unplayable. Harmonica screws are often made of brass, so remember that these are much softer than the steel or iron screws you may be used to handling.

Your weekly clean doesn't need the addition of soap - plain lukewarm water is enough to remove any build-up from the comb and reed-plates. A bottle of spray alcohol will give you all the cleaning material you need for a full clean. Alternatively, fill a small bowl or tupperware with isopropyl (rubbing) alcohol and let your cover and reed-plates soak. Make sure the pieces are completely submerged if you do this. A tupperware is a great option for this method, as you can close the lid to escape the alcohol fumes. Let your cover and reed plates soak for 30 minutes to an hour. While they're soaking, you can wash or brush the comb.

If you choose to spray-clean the cover plates, be sure to clean both the inside (for sanitation) and the outside (for looks). If your comb is made of plastic or metal, you can clean this with alcohol as well. Make sure that any cloth you use to wipe down your harmonica is lint-free. Cloths made for cleaning eyeglasses are great for this purpose (How to Clean and Seal a Harmonica, 2020b).

Always handle exposed reeds with care when you're cleaning. Though they're made of metal, they're extremely delicate and are all too easy to break. Broken or bent reeds are the most common casualty of harmonica cleaning, especially if it's your first time. And replacing reeds is a costly business—so costly that it's cheaper to buy a new harmonica. Make sure that you have a back-up harmonica ready to go before taking apart your favorite instrument for its yearly deep-clean.

It's also very easy to knock the reeds out of alignment when cleaning them, which can cause the harmonica to fall out of tune. Always clean the reeds lengthwise, never brush or rub them from side-to-side. Do not use a brush to clean the reed-plate, as the bristles of the brush can damage the reeds. Instead, use a cloth to wipe down the reed plates, and save the brush for the comb (*Cleaning Your Lee Oskar Harmonica*, 2017).

Make sure that every single part of the harmonica is *completely* dry before putting it back together. This doesn't just refer to water droplets. Playing your harmonica before the alcohol has fully dried can cause you to inhale alcohol fumes when you play, which can be extremely dangerous.

Chapter 8:
Glossary of Terms

A-M

ABS

Plastic material that is often used for making the comb of a harmonica.

Airtight

Harmonicas are specifically built to prevent air from leaking out between the reed plates and the comb.

Amplifier

Electronic harmonicas can be connected to an amplifier.

Bending

Lowering the naturally played pitch of a reed caused by altering slightly the pressure of the breath passing over the reed. On a C harmonica, draw notes are bent on holes 1–6, and blow notes are bent on holes 7–10,

Blow

These are notes that are made by exhaling. The blow notes are created by the upper reeds where the reeds open inside the harmonica.

Chamber

Opening in the comb into which the reeds vibrate. The outer holes of the chambers are the open holes that form the mouthpiece.

Chromatic

Tuning that uses all 12 notes.

Chromatic Harmonica

Chromatic harmonicas have a slide activated by a button that changes the reed that is sounded to enable full chromatic play.

Comb

The comb is the central piece of the harmonica. This is the part of the harmonica that you blow air through. Combs can be made of wood, plastic, or metal.

Closing Bend

Pitch-lowering bend where the reed is pushed into its slot.

Cover plates

Outer covers of a harmonica. Removing the cover plates will expose the reeds and the reed plates.

Cross Harp

Otherwise known as 2nd position, this is the most common position for rock and blues music.

Cup

The seal formed between the hands and the harmonica.

Diatonic

Tuning that uses only the eight notes from a major or minor scale. This is the tuning for normal 10-hole harmonicas.

Diatonic Harmonica

A 10-hole harmonica tuned to a specific musical key, which is typically displayed somewhere on the top or side of the harmonica.

Discrete

Diatonic harmonica comb with an individual chamber for each reed.

Draw

Notes that are made by inhaling. Draw notes are created by the lower reeds where the reeds open outside the harmonica.

Gap

Space between the reed and its slot in the reed plate.

Embouchure

The way a player applies their lips and tongue to the harmonica.

Harp

May originate from the early term "French harp." This term refers to the harmonica itself (Chrapka, 2018g).

High Harmonica

A diatonic harmonica tuned to play one octave higher than normal.

Key

The musical scale in which the music of a song is written.

Low Harmonica

A diatonic harmonica tuned to a key below G. G is normally considered the "lowest" possible key.

Microphone

Many electric harmonicas come equipped with a microphone to amplify the sound (*Harmonica jargon simplified and explained - All you need to know about the harmonica <<Eagle music shop blog,* 2012).

N-Z

Octave

The interval from one note to its respective note is either higher or lower (an octave above or an octave below). The seven notes in the musical alphabet are A, B, C, D, E, F, G. When the same note repeats itself at a higher or lower pitch, it has jumped up or down one octave.

Opening Bend

Pitch-raising bend where the reed slides away from its slot.

Overblow

Type of bend that plays the opposite reed in an opening fashion. Overblows raise the pitch of the note, while normal bends lower it. On a C harmonica, overblows can be made on holes 1–6, and overdraws can be made on holes 7–10.

Position

Indicates the starting place (hole number) and manner (draw or blow) in which the root note of the scale is played. When played in different positions, the harmonica takes on different characteristic sounds.

Reeds

Thin, rectangular metal strips (normally brass) attached to a mounting plate that springs back and forth through its slot when the player blows or draws air through the harmonica. This is what produces the harmonica's sound.

Reed plates

Mounting plates for the harmonica's reeds.

Resonance

Amplification due to sound waves echoing and superimposing.

Retuning

The process of realigning old reeds to bring the harmonica back into tune.

Richter Tuning

This is considered the "standard" tuning in which most harmonicas are arranged. This is named after Joseph Richter, who invented this tuning method.

Rivets

The small metal pieces used to fasten the reeds to the reed plates.

Slide

The button-activated mechanism within a chromatic harmonica that changes the reed being sounded.

Slot

A hole in the reed plate slightly larger than its reed. The reed vibrates through the slot to produce sound.

Solo-Tuning

A specialized tuning that changes the normal diatonic notation layout to include the fourth and sixth notes of the scale. These notes are omitted in the Richter tuning.

Tab

Notation that indicates how to play a note on the harmonica.

Tremolo

Fluctuations in air pressure that cause a wavering effect to the loudness of the sound.

Tremolo Harmonica

A tremolo harmonica has two reeds for each note.

Valves

Sometimes called "windsavers," these are specialized plastic flaps that cover the reed slots in chromatic harmonicas.

Vibrato

Changes of pitch produced by a slight wavering movement of part of the embouchure affecting the air stream (Chrapka, 2018g).

Wood

Traditional combs are made of wood. While wooden combs are still fashionable in contemporary harmonicas, they are also noted for having a short life and several maintenance problems (*Harmonica jargon simplified and explained - All you need to know about the harmonica <<Eagle music shop blog,* 2012).

Conclusion

When you first opened this book, you may have thought of the harmonica as a simple shiny box that makes music. You may have cringed at the idea of music theory or believed that learning a musical instrument was beyond your talent or budget. Now you have an intimate understanding of what the harmonica is and how it plays music. You have all the knowledge that you need to make an informed purchase, and once that purchase is made, you have the proper technique for cleaning and maintaining your new instrument. You know the difference between a diatonic and a chromatic scale. You understand the difference between musical keys, you know the difference between a half-step and a whole step, and you may even have begun sounding out the notes on your own harmonica.

Whether you've been playing along or decided to read the book all the way through before sounding your first note, you're far more knowledgeable now than you were just yesterday. And no matter how thorough or clear my technical explanations may have been, you'll find that there's an entire world to uncover when you begin playing the harmonica seriously.

This book is just a starting point, but you can also think of it as a roadmap or a user's manual. The techniques and information contained in this book are just here to get you started. Once you've mastered the songs, techniques, postures, and scales in this book, you'll be delighted to find that there are many places you can go with this humble little instrument. However, as you become more confident in your playing, you can rest in the knowledge that you'll always have this book on-hand for reference, should you need it. If you ever find yourself struggling to remember what "slant harp" means or what's the difference between a chromatic and tremolo harmonica, you can always refer back to this book to bring you up to speed. If you run into trouble cleaning or want to try your hand at tuning up your harmonica, you have that knowledge within easy reach. Whatever questions or concerns you may have in the future, you now have a simple guide to the basics that you can refer back to whenever you need to refresh your knowledge.

I hope that this book not only unlocks a deep love of the harmonica within you but a deep love of music in general. The musical theory contained in this book doesn't just apply to the harmonica. You can take it with you to any future instruments that you may attempt to play. If you find yourself deeply immersed in a particular genre, you may find yourself wishing to branch out into the other musical instruments within that genre, or even find yourself discovering more musical artists within a genre that you love. I hope that, after reading this book and practicing every day with your harmonica, you can look at other people in the eye and tell them with pride that you are a *musician*.

References

8 Tips for How to Bend on Harmonica. (n.d.). Tomlin Harmonica Lessons. https://www.tomlinharmonicalessons.com/8-tips-for-how-to-bend-on-harmonica/

Allen, J. P. (n.d.). *How to Make Your Harmonica Last a Long Time*. Harmonica. https://www.harmonica.com/harmonica-maintenance-cleaning-594.html

Berloto, B. (2020, June 16). *How to read Harmonica Tabs*. Lecciones de Armónica. https://www.leccionesdearmonica.com/en/blog/8581/how-to-read-harmonica-tabs/

Best for Beginners: Exploring Three Harmonica Types. (n.d.). Harmonica. https://www.harmonica.com/types-of-harmonica-7325.html

Best Harmonica Beginner's Guide with TOP 10 Harmonica Reviews 2020. (2020, January 8). Wind Plays. https://windplays.com/best-harmonicas/

Care and Maintenance of a Harmonica. (n.d.). Yamaha. https://www.yamaha.com/en/musical_instrument_guide/harmonica/maintenance/

Chrapka, C. (2018a, May 2). *Harmonica Embouchures*. TheMusicStand. https://www.themusicstand.ca/blogs/htp-harmonica/embouchures

Chrapka, C. (2018b, May 3). *Playing Notes with Your Harmonica*. The Music Stand. https://www.themusicstand.ca/blogs/htp-harmonica/playing-notes

Chrapka, C. (2018c, May 4). *Bending Notes with the Harmonica*. The Music Stand. https://www.themusicstand.ca/blogs/htp-harmonica/bending

Chrapka, C. (2018d, May 5). *How to Breathe When Playing Harmonica*. The Music Stand. https://www.themusicstand.ca/blogs/htp-harmonica/breathe

Chrapka, C. (2018e, May 7). *Parts of a Harmonica*. The Music Stand. https://www.themusicstand.ca/blogs/htp-harmonica/parts

Chrapka, C. (2018f, May 8). *How Does the Harmonica Work?* The Music Stand. https://www.themusicstand.ca/blogs/htp-harmonica/work

Chrapka, C. (2018g, May 9). *Basic Harmonica Definitions*. The Music Stand.https://www.themusicstand.ca/blogs/htp-harmonica/definitions

Derhgawen, A. (n.d.). *Harmonica Positions Explained*. Harmonica.https://www.harmonica.com/harmonica-keys-positions-19.html

Eyers, T. (n.d.). *Harmonica Notes – What are the notes on a harmonica?* Harmonica Tunes. http://harmonicatunes.com/harmonica-notes/

Fix Your Harmonica. (n.d.). Hohner.De. https://www.hohner.de/en/service/harmonica/clean-maintain

How to Choose a Harmonica. (2018, October 1). Musician's Friend. https://www.musiciansfriend.com/thehub/harmonica-buying-guide

Great Songs to Play on Harmonica. (n.d.). ArtistWorks. https://my.artistworks.com/blog/great-songs-play-harmonica

Harmonica jargon simplified and explained – all you need to know about the harmonica. (2012, December 26). Eagle Music Shop. https://www.eaglemusicshop.com/blog/harmonica-jargon-simplified-and-explained-all-you-need-to-know-abou-the-harmonica/

Harmonica Tabs: 100s of the Most Popular Songs Ever. (n.d.). Harmonica. https://www.harmonica.com/harmonica-tabs-songs-28144.html

Harmonica/Music Style. (n.d.). Wikibooks. https://en.wikibooks.org/wiki/Harmonica/Music_Style

Hertzberg, F. (2020, April 5). *Recommendations for Buying Harmonicas*. Blues Harmonica Kaizen. https://fredrikhertzberg.com/harmonica-gear/recommendations-for-buying-harmonicas/

How to Clean a Harmonica. (n.d.). The Harmonica Company. https://theharmonicacompany.com/how-to-clean-harmonica/?v=79cba1185463

Cleaning Your Lee Oskar Harmonica. (2017, December 15). Lee Oskar Harmonicas. https://leeoskar.com/ufaqs/how-to-clean-your-harmonica/

How to Play the Harmonica. (2020a, July 27). https://www.instructables.com/id/How-To-Play-The-Harmonica/

How to Clean and Seal a Harmonica. (2020b, August 21). Instructables. https://www.instructables.com/id/How-to-clean-a-harmonica/

Leonhardt, S. (2020, February 25). *How to Hold a Harmonica*. Musical Instrument Guide. https://musicalinstrumentguide.com/how-to-hold-a-harmonica/

How a Harmonica Works. (2019, April 12). Making Music Magazine. https://makingmusicmag.com/how-a-harmonica-works/

Octave Harmonicas. (n.d.). Harmonicas Direct. https://harmonicas-direct.com/product-category/harmonicas/octave-harmonicas/

Old MacDonald had a farm – harmonica song for kids. (n.d.). Harmonica Tabs. https://harmonica-tabs.com/old-macdonald-had-a-farm-harmonica-song-for-kids/

The Structure of the Harmonica: Learn the names of the parts. (n.d.). Yamaha. https://www.yamaha.com/en/musical_instrument_guide/harmonica/mechanism/

The Ultimate Guide to Harmonicas for Curious Newbies. (2020, May 10). E-Home Recording Studio. https://ehomerecordingstudio.com/best-harmonicas/

Today's 20 Most Popular Songs. (n.d.). Harptabs.com. https://www.harptabs.com/

Understanding 1st/2nd Position: Two Basic Styles of Playing. (2019, April 4). Lee Oskar Harmonicas. https://leeoskar.com/ufaqs/understanding-1st-2nd-position/

What Are Harmonica Tabs or Harmonica Tablature? (2020, August 10). Harmonica. https://support.harmonica.com/article/82-what-are-harmonica-tabs-or-harmonica-tablature

What Are Positions on Harmonica? (2020, March 4). Tomlin Harmonica Lessons. https://www.tomlinharmonicalessons.com/what-are-positions-on-harmonica/

Which Harmonica to Buy? (n.d.). HarmonicaLessons.com. https://www.harmonicalessons.com/beginner-which-harmonica-to-buy.html

Which Keys of Harmonica Should I Buy to Get Started? (2017, December 26). Lee Oskar Harmonicas. https://leeoskar.com/ufaqs/which-keys-should-i-buy/

Whitner, G. (2020, July 19). *Best Harmonicas for Beginners in 2020 – A Mouthful of Joy.* Music Oomph. https://musicoomph.com/best-harmonicas/

Yerxa, W. (2016a, March 26). *How a Harmonica Works.* dummies. https://www.dummies.com/art-center/music/harmonica/how-a-harmonica-works/

Yerxa, W. (2016b, March 26). *How to Care for Your Harmonica.* dummies. https://www.dummies.com/art-center/music/harmonica/how-to-care-for-your-harmonica/

Yerxa, W. (2016c, March 26). *How to Play Your First Bend on the Harmonica.* dummies. https://www.dummies.com/art-center/music/harmonica/how-to-play-your-first-bend-on-the-harmonica/

Yerxa, W. (2016d, March 26). *How to Project Your Harmonica Sound with Your Hands.* dummies. https://www.dummies.com/art-center/music/harmonica/how-to-project-your-harmonica-sound-with-your-hands/

Yerxa, W. (2016e, March 26). *How to Tune Your Harmonica.* dummies. https://www.dummies.com/art-center/music/harmonica/how-to-tune-your-harmonica/

Yerxa, W. (2016f, March 26). *Tips for Buying Your First Harmonica.* dummies. https://www.dummies.com/art-center/music/harmonica/tips-for-buying-your-first-harmonica/

Yerxa, W. (2020, July 7). *Harmonica for Dummies Cheat Sheet.* dummies. https://www.dummies.com/art-center/music/harmonica/harmonica-for-dummies-cheat-sheet/